Potomac Heritage Trail

A HIKER'S GUIDE

*A National Scenic Trail Connecting the Tidewater Potomac
to the Forks of the Ohio River in Pittsburgh*

HIKE DATA,
TRIP PLANNERS,
EXPLORING
OPTIONS,
RESOURCES
AND MORE!

D0886270

POTOMAC HERITAGE
NATIONAL SCENIC TRAIL

BY David Edwin Lillard & Ed Talone

ACKNOWLEDGEMENTS
This book was produced by the Allegheny Trail Alliance with assistance
from the American Hiking Society and support from the National Park
Service Challenge Cost-Share Program and Potomac Heritage National
Scenic Trail Office.

PHOTOS: Public domain except where noted
DESIGN: Apollo Design Group, Latrobe, Pa.
MAPS: Karen T. Zachary and National Park Service
PRINTER: Laurel Valley Graphics, Latrobe, Pa.

Table of Contents

SAFETY

Hiking activities will always involve a certain amount of risk, for which you assume responsibility. We can not be held responsible for any accidents, encounters, or problems you may experience on the trail. While we have been as accurate as possible in this book concerning trail conditions, trail conditions do change over time, as a result of the weather, and as the trail system continues to grow.

Potomac Heritage Trail

A HIKER'S GUIDE

Most of us are accustomed to thinking of trails as unbroken, continuous pathways from one place to another. Perhaps one day we will experience the Potomac Heritage National Scenic Trail (PHT) in this way. But even then, how many of us, in any given year, will lace up our boots and walk 770 miles of trails and roadsides? Some intrepid hikers will, but others will want to explore the trail corridor in a more leisurely manner. The Potomac River already provides a continuous thread over much of the corridor's length. Just as early Americans saw the trail corridor as a passage connecting the Chesapeake Bay with lands beyond the Allegheny Mountains, today we use some of the same routes as pathways to discovery. Depending on your interests, the trail corridor can reveal the stories of American roots, music, industrial history, natural history, the nation's outdoor-recreation heritage, military history and more. You don't have to cover every inch of the trail corridor to experience its richness. But you can, by using this guide.

WHAT'S IN THIS GUIDEBOOK

This first edition of a hiking guide to the Potomac Heritage National Scenic Trail corridor covers the Northern Virginia, Maryland, Washington, D.C., and Pennsylvania sections of the PHT. New segments in Tidewater Virginia and Southern Maryland are being developed by local and state agencies and will be added to future editions of this guide.

The Potomac Heritage National Scenic Trail (PHT) is an evolving, 770-mile network of locally-managed trails and routes embracing both sides of the Potomac from the mouth of the river at the Chesapeake Bay to the Allegheny Highlands in the upper Ohio River basin. Trails in the Maryland/D.C./Pennsylvania segments of the trail corridor make it possible to hike 375 miles from Washington, D.C. to Seward, Pennsylvania and Allegheny County, Pennsylvania—all on trails and sidewalks. South of Washington, D.C., there are many places that offer superb hiking, with more opportunities on the horizon.

On the Virginia side of the Potomac River, local PHT advocates are bringing into focus a continuous footpath between Prince William Forest

Park and Whites Ferry near Leesburg, Virginia, a distance of about 70 miles. Hikers will be able to cross the Potomac on the ferry and either continue north on the C&O Canal Towpath or head south toward Georgetown to complete a loop.

South of Prince William, in the area of Fredericksburg and in Virginia's historic Northern Neck, hiking opportunities in PHT corridor are plentiful. To complement such adventures, guides for bicycling and paddling routes entice further exploration of the Potomac and its streams and landscapes.

The route on the northern side of the Potomac begins at Point Lookout State Park. Although the amount of "roadside walking" in Southern Maryland makes a continuous route impractical for most people, this guide gives you the information needed to do it. More importantly, the route in this guide will deliver you to some of the best places to experience the Potomac on foot—even if you're getting from one hike to the next by car or bicycle. Recent land purchases along the river by local, state and federal agencies will add many miles of trail in tidewater areas. Even now, the corridor offers a scenic and relaxed roadside walk.

In Washington, D.C., the path follows a route connecting the Fort Circle Parks, which also provides interludes in Rock Creek and Glover-Archbold Parks. Woven together, these trails create a world-class urban hiking experience.

Upstream from Georgetown in the District of Columbia, the towpath within the Chesapeake & Ohio Canal National Historical Park stretches 184.5 miles west through the Piedmont, Blue Ridge and Ridge and Valley provinces to Cumberland, Maryland. From here, the Somerset County section of the Great Allegheny Passage takes the trail into the town of Frostburg, then through Big Savage Mountain, into the town of Meyersdale, and on to the town of Confluence and the Youghiogheny River. In Ohiopyle State Park, the Youghiogheny River Trail South (YRTS) section of the Great Allegheny Passage meets the 70-mile Laurel Highlands Hiking Trail, which follows Laurel Ridge northeast to the town of Seward. Or, from Ohiopyle, hikers can continue northwest on the YRTS and other trails in the Great Allegheny Passage trail system into Pittsburgh.

THE HIKES

In this guidebook, the trail is divided into six sections. Each section is divided into hikes. We call them hikes whether they follow trails, sidewalks or roads. At the end of the book, there is a chapter on additional trail resources and one that lists some ideas for further reading. Here is what you will find in each section.

Map. Most sections are introduced by a map of the entire section. The maps do not offer detailed illustration of the lay of the land. Other agencies and organizations are already doing a great job of that. Rather, our maps help you get to the trail, offer basic navigational points relative to trail heads and roadways, and help you find some of the interesting sites along the way. Sections without maps are 5, 7 and 9.

Description. Each section is introduced with an overview of the route, including a description of the surrounding terrain, proximity to water, whether you will follow road or trail, and a little bit of history.

Hikes. Each hike chapter has easy-to-read headings to help you prepare, navigate and enjoy the journey.

Hike Number. The hikes range in length from several miles to more than 20. Dividing them into hikes is just a convenient way to divide the book. You can find a short hike within even the longest ones in the guide. As a bonus, there are descriptions of hiking destinations on Virginia's Northern Neck, where a PHT route is still under development.

Local Trail Name. Trail segments along the PHT are managed by a variety of entities through which the trail passes. You can find contact information for the segments and volunteer organizations that support them in the Resources section of this guide.

Start and End Points. Each start and end point is located where you can find parking or access by public transportation.

Trip Planner. At the beginning of each section, the planner offers the information you need to pick and plan a hike. It includes the length of the hike in miles, cultural sites, parks and resource areas intersected, significant natural history features, trail intersections, parking areas, locations for water and sanitary facilities, camping opportunities on or near the trail in this section, and a few notes on lodging and dining.

Hike Data. This is a brief table that lists milestones of the section, focusing primarily on navigational information.

Explore the Potomac Heritage Trail Corridor. Following the hike data are notes on a few destination sites on or near the trail.

Resources. At the end of each section, you will find a listing of organizations and agencies that may be able to provide additional information to plan your trip.

Trail Resources and Outdoor Contacts. This chapter provides contact information on a wider range of resources than are listed in each section of the guide. It includes land trusts that are active in the corridor, hiking clubs, outdoor education groups, and other people who, either directly or indirectly, enable us all to enjoy the heritage of the trail corridor.

Further Reading About Potomac Heritage. This is a grab bag of books, periodicals and websites. Some of them are gateways to more experiences and some of them offer deep exploration in the history, ecology and culture of the Potomac.

SOUTHERN MARYLAND

The route from Point Lookout, at the mouth of the Potomac River, to Oxon Cove Park, just south of Washington, D.C., is covered in six hikes. Most of the hiking and walking opportunities are separated by significant stretches of roadway—ground most people will cover by car in ten to fifteen minute interludes. While this is not the traditional way of traveling a trail, it allows more time for stopping at farmstands and heritage sites, compared to bicycling or hiking. It also provides more time for exploring the parks and sites along the route, rather than merely passing through them. You can make an easy two or three day outing by bicycling the road walks and exploring the many natural areas and heritage sites on foot.

However you travel, you will never be far from water. Nanjemoy Creek and the Saint Mary's, Wicomico and Port Tobacco Rivers define the region and tell the stories of colonial America's earliest days. Traveling north toward Washington, D.C., you discover that Southern Maryland's heritage is more than stories of colonial times. Nature is the star of the show, featuring shore grasses, wide river mouths, and wildlife characteristic of the Chesapeake Bay.

Contrasted with the tumbling tributaries upriver and the rugged mountains where the Potomac Heritage National Scenic Trail traces high into the Allegheny Mountains, you can see that the trail and the river are the threads of continuity among the several million people who live in the region.

Two other influences on the landscape are noteworthy: the U.S. military and Native Americans. Military installations have been present almost for as long as the European settlers. The Patuxent River Naval Air Station and the U.S. Naval Surface Warfare Center at Indian Head and Stump Neck are major features of the culture and local economy. Interestingly, some of the largest natural areas of Southern Maryland are adjacent to the bases.

In Southern Maryland there is an abundance of places and streams bearing names such as Nanjemoy, Mattawoman, Wicomoco, Chicamuxen. The best known people of the area were the Conoy, also called the Piscataway for the village they inhabited on the river. They spoke an Algonquian language and were closely related to the Nanticoke of the Chesapeake's Eastern Shore and the Kanawha of West Virginia. The

Patuxent, whose main village was in today's Calvert County, also were also associated with the Conoy.

The Potawomeck, Wicomoco, and others in the Powhatan confederacy from the Virginia side of the river came as visitors and appear to have been prolific place namers. According to the chronicles of Captain John Smith's exploration of 1608, the place names they offered up are some of the ones that survive today—albeit in forms transformed through time.

The Susquehanna, who spoke an Iroquois language, pushed into the region in the mid-seventeenth century, warring with the Piscataway people, colonists, and just about everyone else. Their history lies primarily north along the river that bears their name. Their arrival to the Potomac coincided with the early days of English settlement.

The word Potomac has been ascribed various meanings. Among them are "bring into" and "where they are brought to." One that seems appropriate today is "where they come together, " or gathering place. The lower Potomac has long been such a place. It drew the original peoples to fish, and the settlers to farm and trade. And it has attracted generations of Americans to enjoy the natural beauty of the river, its tributaries and the landscape.

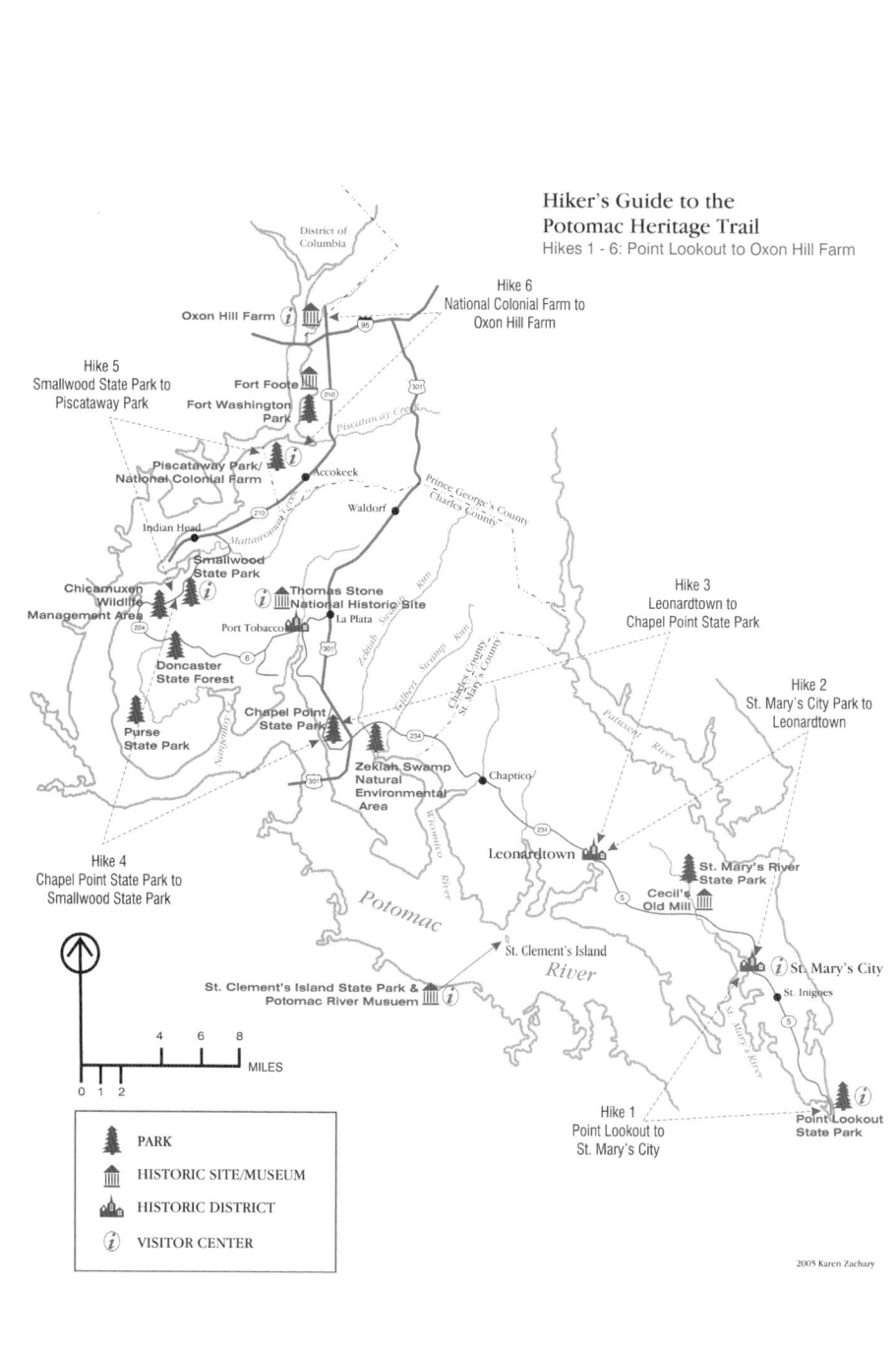

Hiker's Guide to the
Potomac Heritage Trail
Hikes 1 - 6: Point Lookout to Oxon Hill Farm

District of
Columbia

Hike 6
National Colonial Farm to
Oxon Hill Farm

Oxon Hill Farm

Hike 5
Smallwood State Park to
Piscataway Park

Fort Foote
Fort Washington Park

Piscataway Park/
National Colonial Farm

Accokeek

Indian Head

Waldorf

Prince George's County
Charles County

Smallwood State Park

Chicamuxen
Wildlife
Management Area

Thomas Stone
National Historic Site

Port Tobacco

La Plata

Hike 3
Leonardtown to
Chapel Point State Park

Doncaster
State Forest

Hike 2
St. Mary's City Park to
Leonardtown

Purse
State Park

Chapel Point
State Park

Charles County
St. Mary's County

Zekiah Swamp
Natural
Environmental
Area

Chaptico

Hike 4
Chapel Point State Park to
Smallwood State Park

Leonardtown

St. Mary's River
State Park

Cecil's
Old Mill

Potomac

St. Clement's Island

River

St. Mary's City

St. Clement's Island State Park &
Potomac River Museum

St. Inigoes

4   6   8

MILES

0 1 2

Hike 1
Point Lookout to
St. Mary's City

Point Lookout
State Park

PARK

HISTORIC SITE/MUSEUM

HISTORIC DISTRICT

VISITOR CENTER

2005 Karen Zachary

Hike 1
Point Lookout to Historic St. Mary's City

The PHT in Maryland begins at Point Lookout, a peninsula that forms the dramatic confluence of the Potomac River and Chesapeake Bay. Beginning at the lighthouse on Point Lookout, the trail follows a mile of sandy beach before meandering through the interior of Point Lookout State Park. There are views of Cornfield Harbor and Point Lookout Creek a short walk from the visitor center. Then comes a jaunt along a Civil War-era railroad bed through quiet marsh. Outside the park, the trail begins a long, but pleasant road walk to St. Mary's City.

TRIP PLANNER

Start: Point Lookout, at Maryland's mouth of the Potomac River.

End: St. Mary's City.

Miles: 13. 9

Points of Interest: Point Lookout State Park, Ferry to Smith Island, a rail-trail through marshland, Circle C Oyster Ranch, Saint Ignatius Chapel, St. Mary's City.

Parking: Point Lookout (0.1 mi.), Ridge, Md. post office (8.4 mi.), St. Mary's City (13.9 mi.).

Water: Point Lookout State Park, Saint Inigoes Landing, St. Mary's City.

Restroom or Privy: Point Lookout, St. Mary's City.

Provisions: Grocery store (Raley's) in Ridge, three seafood restaurants on Wynne Road.

Camping: Point Lookout State Park, Seaside View Campground.

HIKE DATA

0.0   Point Lookout Lighthouse. Walk west on Route 5 past smokehouse.

0.1   Leave Route 5 at the parking area, turn left onto beach. Turn right on the path along a stone wall. At the end of the stone wall, continue north on beach.

0.6   Leaving the beach (50 yd. before the jetty), turn right into woods on a path. Emerging from the woods, continue on the sandy path toward footbridge.

0.7   Cross a footbridge into the parking area for boat launches and the ferry to Smith Island.

0.9   Turn left on Route 5.

1.3   Turn left onto a wooded path, leaving Route 5, entering Point Lookout State Park campground. Follow campground access loops to the visitor center. The park offers tent sites and camper sites. Campground registration cabin is at the main entrance to the park, 0.2 mi. further up Route 5.

1.9   Visitor center. Join the nature trail behind the building.

2.0   Point Lookout Rail Trail. Turn right. The railroad was constructed in 1866, but never completed. For an intimate view of the bay, turn left for a detour on the rail trail, and walk 175 yards to the vista.

2.5   Turn right at second path to campground, leaving the rail trail. Follow a sandy path; stay left at the fork in the reeds.

2.6   Rejoin campground loop; turn right. Then bear left toward Route 5.

2.7   Turn left on Route 5.

3.5   At T intersection, bear left at Memorial. Continue on Route 5.

5.6   Ridge, Md.; Post Office, groceries, gasoline, on right.

5.7   Airedale Road. Turn right and follow to end (approximately .75 mile) to visit Circle C Oyster Ranch.

9.4   Saint Peter Claver Road. Turn left for Cardinal Gibbons Park (playground, tennis and basketball courts) or Seaside View Campground.

10.9   Villa Road, Saint Inigoes, Md. Turn left and continue 1.6 miles to Saint Ignatius Church.

13.9   Turn left on Rosecroft Road into St. Mary's City. Turn right onto Hogaboom Lane and park. Enter the visitor center to pay admission and acquire trail maps and other information.

EXPLORING THE PHT

Point Lookout State Park. Point Lookout is a peninsula situated at point where the Potomac River empties into the Chesapeake Bay, and affords a rare simultaneous view of both. After Captain John Smith explored the Point, it was included in King Charles I's 1632 grant to George Calvert, Lord Baltimore. Calvert's younger son, Leonard, claimed the Point for his home in 1634, after being named Maryland's first governor. The Point played a role in each war fought on American soil. During the American Revolution and War of 1812, it served as a lookout point. During the Civil War, it became a prisoner of war camp for captured Confederate soldiers.

Local legend claims the historic lighthouse and prisoner camp are haunted, and the park hosts a Ghost Walk every October. The 1,046 acre state park offers swimming, boating, fishing, and camping at both tent and trailer sites. There also are rustic cabins and a cottage available by reservation. The visitor center houses a Civil War museum and nature exhibits.

Ferry to Smith Island. Take a cruise to Smith Island, Maryland's only inhabited island in the Chesapeake Bay. Departing from the marina in Point Lookout State Park, the ferry takes visitors to one of the last outposts of quiet in the eastern U.S. Few residents have cars on the island, and visitors leave theirs on the mainland to stroll the island's three communities. There are B&Bs and a couple of hotels, the Smith Island Center museum and cultural center, a few eateries, and views of the Bay at every turn. Cruises available from the end of May through Mid-October, costing about $20 per person.

Ridge. The concentration of restaurants at the end of Wynne Road is a testament to the quality of local fish and the long-standing persistence of the watermen's culture in this southern portion of St. Mary's County. From Route 5, turn left onto Wynne Road and travel two miles to the end, where you will meet up again with a lovely view of the Potomac and be able to choose between three locally owned waterfront restaurants specializing in delicious Potomac seafood.

Saint Ignatius Church. At the end of Villa Road in the small rural hamlet of Saint Inigoes, this chapel, on the National Register of Historic Places, is the oldest continuously occupied Jesuit property in the United States. The original 1641 church was removed in the 18th century, then rebuilt after the American Revolution. It houses one of the oldest cemeteries in America. The adjacent guard gate for the Patuxent River Naval Air Station on Webster's Field makes for an interesting cultural contrast. (301) 972-5590.

Hike 2
St. Mary's City to Leonardtown

The first four miles of this section lie entirely within Historic St. Mary's City, following the park system of footpaths through the recreated town that served as Maryland's first capital. Wooded paths lead to dramatic views of the St. Mary's River and sites undergoing archaeological exploration. Most people will cover the segment that follows, between St. Mary's and Leonardtown, on bicycle or by car. This strategy allows time for a hike around Saint Mary's Lake and a leisurely lunch and stroll in old Leonardtown.

TRIP PLANNER

Start: St. Mary's City.
End: Chapel Point State Park.
Miles: 19.2
Points of Interest: Historic St. Mary's City, St. Mary's River Lake, Historic Leonardtown.
Parking: Historic St. Mary's City (13.9 mi.), Leonardtown (23.9).
Water: Historic St. Mary's City, Take it Easy Campground, La Grand Estate Camping Resort.
Restroom or Privy: Historic St. Mary's City, various businesses along Route 5, Leonardtown business establishments.
Provisions: Various businesses along the Route 5 road walk.
Camping: Take it Easy Campground; La Grande Estate Camping Resort.

HIKE DATA

0.0   From the parking area on Hogaboom Road, walk south 75 yards to Rosecrost Road. Turn right

0.4   Godiah Spray Tobacco Plantation. Turn right.

0.5   Turn left on Robert Ridgeley Trail; enter woods.

1.1   Emerge from woods, cross the road into woods, with Lucas Road on the right.

1.5   Stay right at post, circle field, cross parking area.

1.7   End of parking lot. Turn right and proceed down a dirt path. The side trail at the end of lot leads 100 yards to a view of St. Mary's River.

2.0   Rejoin Rosecroft Road; continue straight ahead.

2.3   Turn left on unpaved Hogaboom Road.

2.6   Visitor center parking area. From the water fountain, with buildings on right, descend steps toward paths. Turn left onto Town Center

Path. For an alternate route along a dirt path, from the parking area, turn left onto Key Swamp Trail—which rejoins Town Center Path at Print House Path.

2.7   Junction with Print House Path. Turn left on dirt path.

3.0   Turn left onto Aldermanbury Street.

4.0   Maryland Dove exhibit. Snacks, restrooms, exhibits, and unique gift shop. Continue straight on path to the State House.

4.2   Reach the State House. Follow the path around the building, turn left on Old State House Road, then immediately right onto Trinity Church Road.

4.3   Turn left onto Route 5. You can visit the campus center of St. Mary's College by turning right onto Route 5 and following the crosswalk onto the brick path.

10.5 Reach junction with Route 471, Indian Bridge Road. Stay left on Route 5. (For an alternate route, turn right on Route 471 and follow 4.5 mi. to Route 4. Turn left and walk 3.6 mi. to rejoin Route 5 just south of Leonardtown.). Cecil's Old Mill Museum and Shop are 0.3 miles past this intersection on Indian Bridge Road.

11.5 Route 249; Take It Easy Campground is on the left.

12.7 Camp Cosomo Road. For a side trip to St. Mary's Lake, turn right and follow the road 1.2 miles.

15.5 Redgate Wilderness, La Grande Estate Camping Resort.

18.3 Route 4 enters from right.

18.7 Turn left on Business Route 5.

19.2 Leonardtown, Md., business district. Turn right onto Washington Street. There is a sandwich shop, restaurants and a motel in town. Follow Washington Street. down the hill for a view of Breton Bay.

EXPLORING THE PHT

Historic Saint Mary's City Park. Settled in 1634 by 134 English settlers who accompanied Leonard Calvert across the Atlantic, St. Mary's was the fourth permanent settlement in the Americas. St. Mary's was the Maryland Province's capital until the seat was moved to Annapolis in 1695. The park, situated on the shore of the scenic Saint Mary's River, recreates and interprets early life in the colony. While none of the original buildings survive, the archaeological record is considered one of the finest in the U.S. The reconstructed buildings, plantation, businesses and state capitol are all accessed via a series of footpaths that meander the river and woods.

The route of the PHT in this book winds right through the city. Within the park, a three-mile forested loop beginning at the visitor center visits

Godiah Spray Plantation, Milburn Creek, and Chancellor's Point, crossing small bridges named after some of St. Mary's most notable 17th century personalities. A former plantation home is now a B&B featuring fine dining and distinctive guestrooms, where visitors and passersby can enjoy spectacular views of the St. Mary's River below.

St. Mary's Lake River State Park. The highlight is a 250-acre lake. An eight-mile wooded trail circles the lake, where evidence indicates Native Americans have lived since 3000 B.C. Attentive hikers might encounter arrowheads along stream beds.

Leonardtown. The county seat of St. Mary's, Leonardtown offers a dose of small-town charm and an easy-going pace. The oldest incorporated town in Maryland, Leonardtown is host to a few casual eateries, several shops, an art gallery, a health food store, and accommodations. Tired legs might find the shaded benches in the town center to be the main attraction. The area surrounding the town is fast-growing, but downtown Leonardtown still has the illusion of an isolated, Southern Maryland county seat—only the availability of cappuccino gives it away.

Hike 3
Leonardtown to Chapel Point State Park

This section presents a long road walk—one likely to be traversed on foot in its entirety only by the most serious of through-hikers. With an absence of public camping along the route, this will make for a long day. Most people will want to cover the distance on bicycle or in a car, with stops along the way to enjoy the country scenery and Zekiah Swamp.

As far as road walks go, the saunter down Hurry Road to a crossroads named Hurry pays dividends. It offers views of the surrounding country-side rarely encountered while hiking off-road. The hike is bookended by the quiet village of Leonardtown and the rugged isolation of Chapel Point State Park.

TRIP PLANNER

Start: Leonardtown, Md., at Washington Street and Route 5.
End: Chapel Point State Park.
Miles: 32.4
Points of Interest: Leonardtown, Md., Zekiah Swamp Natural Environment Area, Pope's Creek, Chapel Point State Park.
Parking: Leonardtown (0.0), Chapel Point SP (40.1).
Water: Leonardtown.
Restroom or Privy: Leonardtown business establishments.
Provisions: Various business along the Route 234 road walk.

Camping: None at this time. Motel lodging available where Route 234 meets Route 301.

HIKE DATA

0.0 Leonardtown, Md. Turn right onto Washington Street.

0.3 Route 5. Turn left. There is no shoulder; walk on the grass.

0.6 Pass hospital.

2.3 Junction with Route 234. Turn left.

7.7 Junction Route 242. Turn left.

9.3 Hurry Road. Turn right (no shoulder). To visit Saint Clement's Island, stay straight on 242 and continue for 7.75 miles to the end. It's a bit out of the way, but the flat road en route meanders through beautiful farmland.

12.3 Hurry, Md. Cross Manor Road.

14.4 Route 238. Turn right.

14.5 Route 234. Turn left

18.5 Pass Route 236.

19.3 Enter Charles County.

22.5 Cross Gilbert Swamp Run.

22.9 Allen's Fresh Road. Turn left (no shoulder) and pass through Zekiah Swamp Natural Environment Area.

25.9 Cross Route 301 onto Edge Hill Road.

26.4 Turn right on Pope's Creek Road. There are lovely views of working Southern Maryland farms. There is a narrow shoulder here—walk with caution.

27.4 Turn right at T to stay on Pope's Creek Road.

27.6 Cross Pope's Creek. Look back across the water for a grand view of Governor Nice Memorial Bridge, a two-mile span linking Maryland and Virginia.

30.6 Reach Route 301. Turn left and walk on the shoulder for one mile.

31.6 Turn left on Chapel Point Road. There is no shoulder; use caution.

32.4 Chapel Point State Park; camping by permit.

EXPLORING THE PHT
Leonardtown. See Hike 2 on page 16.

Pope's Creek. John Wilkes Booth crossed the Potomac here after fleeing Ford's Theatre. Pope's Creek is now home to three waterfront crabhouses. The most popular in the region are Gilligan's Pier, (301) 259-4514; Robertson's Crabhouse, (301) 259-0545; Captain Billy's Restaurant, (301) 932-4323. The sunsets alone are worth the trip.

Saint Clement's Island State Park. After a four-month winter journey across the Atlantic in 1634, English colonists traveled up the Potomac and landed at this 40-acre island. It is located a half mile from Colton's Point. You can visit the island on summer weekends by water taxi from Saint Clement's Island-Potomac River Museum. This county museum's attractions include The Little Red Schoolhouse, an early 19th century one-room school that was moved to its current location after more than a hundred years of service. There are also picnic facilities and a fishing pier. Ferries to the island depart Saturdays and Sundays at 12:30 p.m. and 2:30 p.m. Annual events at the Museum include the Potomac Jazz and Seafood Festival and the Blessing of the Fleet, a two-day event featuring food, crafts and fireworks..

Zekiah Swamp. Zekiah Swamp Run is a 21-mile shallow stream through tall grass, more akin to the Everglades than a typical Mid-Atlantic stream. It is the primary headwaters of the Wicomico River—one of nine state-designated scenic rivers, and is considered one of the most significant ecological features in the Chesapeake Bay Watershed. Zekiah Swamp Natural Environment Area is located at the stream's confluence with the Wicomico River. A dirt road departing Allen's Fresh Road, at mile 23.2, leads through the swamp and woods to the Wicomico River. There is no developed trail system. Still, a stroll down the dirt road is memorable.

Chapel Point State Park. Chapel Point State Park, an undeveloped 600-acre multi-use park, is located on the Port Tobacco River. There is a waterfront area that offers excellent fishing and a launch area for canoes and kayaks, as well as a paddle-in campsite; a permit is required. Hikers and campers can encounter quail, white-tailed deer, wild turkey and waterfowl. Currently, there is no developed trail system, but it is easy to ramble the informal paths. Chapel Point is open to hunting in season, and has a small handicap-accessible hunting area. Also, within park boundaries is historic Saint Ignatius Chapel. The view from the grounds of the chapel alone is worth a walk from Washington, D.C.

Hike 4
Chapel Point State Park to Smallwood State Park

Leaving Chapel Point, the route visits places with names nearly as old as Maryland—Port Tobacco, Thomas Stone, Nanjemoy Creek, Tayloe Neck. For now, this section is all road-walking. Recent and planned acquisitions by state and federal agencies, along with existing land owned by the State of Maryland, offer the prospects of a lot of off-road hiking close to the river. As with most of the Southern Maryland PHT, these roads are often wide-shouldered and always full of scenic rewards, whether covered on foot, bicycle or car.

TRIP PLANNER

Start: Chapel Point State Park at Chapel Point Road Trailhead.

End: Smallwood State Park at Route 224.

Miles: 20.6

Points of Interest: Chapel Point State Park, Port Tobacco Historic District, Thomas Stone Historic Site, Doncaster State Demonstration Forest, Smallwood State Park, Mattawoman Creek Art Center.

Parking: Chapel Point State Park (0.0), Port Tobacco (3.1), Doncaster State Forest (12.8), Smallwood State Park (20.6).

Water, Restroom or Privy: Thomas Stone National Historic Site.

Provisions: Various businesses along the Route 5 road walk.

Camping: Chapel Point State Park, Goose Bay Marina and Campground, Smallwood State Park.

HIKE DATA

0.0   Chapel Point State Park. Campsites are available by permit. From Pisces Lane, turn left on Chapel Point Road.

0.7   Cross Megan Lane. This is a narrow stretch of road with reduced visibility. Walk facing traffic.

3.1   Port Tobacco Historic Site.

3.2   Causeway Street. Turn left.

3.4   Route 6, La Plata Road. Turn left. To visit the town of La Plata, turn right on Route 6 and continue 2.5 miles.

3.5   Rosehill Road. To reach Thomas Stone National Historic Site, turn right on Rosehill and go 1.3 mile to the entrance on left.

4.5   Blossom Point Road. To reach Goose Bay camping, follow Blossom Point Road 1.5 mile to Brentland Road. Turn left on Brentland Road. The campground entrance (Goose Bay Lane) is 1 mile on the left.

6.2   Pass through Welcome, Md. Nice wide shoulders.

7.7   Shoulder narrows.

8.3   Continue on Route 6 as it veers right.

10.7   Route 425. Continue straight on Route 6.

12.9   Forest Road, on right. Turn right on Forest Road to visit Doncaster State Forest.

13.9   Junction with Route 344, Chicamuxen Road. Turn right on Route 344. Turn left on Gilroy Road for an alternate entrance to the southern portion of Doncaster Demonstration Forest (there is no signage to guide you).

16.0   Route 344 becomes Route 224. Stay straight on Route 224.

17.2   Chicamuxen Wildlife Management Area. Parking and information available on left.

18.8   Wide shoulders. The going is a little easier here.

20.6   Lucille Thornton Place. Turn left into Smallwood State Park.

EXPLORING THE PHT

Chapel Point State Park. See Hike 3 on page 18.

Chicamuxen Wildlife Management Area. This 381-acre preserve is situated along the Chicamuxen Creek, a Potomac River tributary. Its varied terrain consists of marshlands, rolling woodlands and farm fields. It was the site of a Civil War encampment under the leadership of Union General Joseph Hooker. It's a terrific spot for viewing a variety of waterfowl species such as black ducks, mallards, wood ducks and hooded mergansers. www.dnr.state.md.us/publiclands/southern/chicamuxen.asp.

Port Tobacco Historic District. Historic Port Tobacco Court House is located on Chapel Point Road near the intersection of Route 6 and Chapel Point Road. In 1685 a naval port of entry for the British crown, the town remained a major port through the end of the Revolutionary War. Once the county seat for Charles County, the site was also the location of a Potopaco Indian village. The 1819 Courthouse, 1876 one-room school-house, and museum are open for tours April through October, and other times by appointment.

Thomas Stone National Historic Site. The site preserves the homestead of Thomas Stone, a signer of the Declaration of Independence, and among those framing the Articles of Confederation. Exhibits chronicle archeological information and plantation life in the colonial and federal periods. The facility also contains a bookstore with material focusing on colonial life, the Declaration of Independence, and the Revolutionary War. Footpaths provide the primary access through the estate. www.nps.gov/thst.

La Plata, Md. One of the original railroad towns in Maryland, La Plata inherited the status of Charles County seat from Port Tobacco, and still retains a nostalgic charm while hosting a number of restaurant and shops. Visit on a Wednesday or Saturday and you can stop at the city's seasonal farmers' market.

Doncaster Demonstration Forest. Managed by the State of Maryland, this 1,447 acre demonstration forest offers 13 miles of trails and access roads open to equestrians, hikers, and cross-country skiers, as well as hunters, September through January. Forested picnic areas make a nice stopping point for lunch. Park at the Forest Road entrance and pick up a trail map at the trailer. Call (301) 934-2543 for more information.

Smallwood State Park. This 628-acre park was the homestead of William Smallwood, fourth governor of Maryland and a major general of the Continental Army, the highest-ranking Marylander to serve in the

Revolutionary War. During his governorship, Smallwood was responsible for the arrangement with Virginia which gave Maryland property rights to the Potomac River—a fact that continues to charge the river's waters (politically, legally, and environmentally) to the present day. Smallwood's restored 18th century home, which he called Retreat House, and 19th century tobacco barn are open to public tours on Sundays, May through September. Camping and cabins, some with views of Mattawoman Creek, are available by reservation. Canoes can be rented Wednesdays through Sundays, May through September. There are two miles of hiking trails and a children's playground. From the Marina lot, follow the MCAC signs and arrows to the Mattawoman Creek Art Center, a gallery and gift shop shrouded by tall trees and teeming with eclectic local and national art. The center hosts free workshops, lectures and demonstrations. A contemporary sculpture garden overlooks Mattawoman Creek.

Hike 5
Smallwood State Park to Piscataway Park

Walking toward Washington, D.C., you might expect the access to public conservation lands to diminish. Just the opposite! The PHT follows back roads that visit Maryland's Duncaster Demonstration Forest, Myrtle Grove Wildlife Management Area, Mattawoman Natural Environment Area, and Chapman's Landing Area, which includes the Parris Glendening Natural Environment Area. The hike ends at Piscataway Park—six miles of preserved Potomac shoreline across river from George Washington's Mount Vernon home.

TRIP PLANNER
Start: Smallwood State Park.
End: Piscataway Park.
Miles: 16.4
Points of Interest: Smallwood State Park, Piscataway Park, National Colonial Farm.
Parking: Smallwood State Park (0.0), Piscataway Park (16.1).
Water, Restroom: Smallwood State Park Visitor Center and Museum; Piscataway Park.
Provisions: Shopping center at intersection of Route 210 and Route 227.
Camping: Smallwood State Park.

HIKE DATA
0.0   From Smallwood State Park, turn left on 224 (Chicamuxen Road).
2.3   Begin passing through Mattawoman Natural Environment Area. There are wide shoulders here.

4.5	Turn left on Hawthorne Road, which here is also Routes 224 and 225.
4.9	Junction with Livingston Road, Route 224, on right. For roughly the next 3.5 miles, the trail circles the Parris Glendenning Natural Environment Area and Chapmans Landing State Park. As plans unfold for the area, which was acquired by the State of Maryland in 2002, more off-road trails will emerge.
6.0	Intersection with Route 210, Indian Head Highway. Turn right and follow shoulder.
6.3	Pass Chapmans Landing Road on left. To get off Indian Head Highway for 2.4 miles, turn left and follow Chapman's Landing Road, to where it re-enters the highway.
10.3	Route 227, Marshall Hall Road. Turn left.
12.7	Barry's Hill Road. Turn right.
13.4	Enter Prince George's County.
14.4	Old Marshall Hall Road.
15.6	Cactus Hill Road. Turn right.
16.1	Bryan Point Road. Turn left.
16.4	Entrance to National Colonial Farm. Parking.

EXPLORING THE PHT
Smallwood State Park. See Hike 4 on page 20.
Myrtle Grove Wildlife Management Area. Along Route 225, located at a site once home to the Piscataway Indians, this 1,723-acre preserve is in the forested bottomlands of Mattawoman Creek. The forest habitat of oaks, hickories, maples, sycamores, poplars and beech is home to barred owls, quails, woodcocks, turkeys and mourning doves.
Accokeek Foundation. A nonprofit dedicated to the practice and teaching of land stewardship and sustainable land practices, the Accokeek Foundation is host to three attractions. Together, they explore the interrelation between food, land use, and environmental protection in a historical context, providing opportunities to make comparisons among cultural values of the past, present, and future.
Piscataway Park. Piscataway Park, administered by the National Park Service, was established in 1961 as a pilot project in the use of easements to protect the Mount Vernon viewshed. Today, Piscataway Park covers approximately 5,000 acres, and stretches for six miles from Piscataway Creek to Marshall Hall on the Potomac River. A place of great natural beauty, Piscataway Park is home to bald eagles, beavers, deer, fox, osprey and many other species. The park has a public fishing pier and two boardwalks over fresh water tidal wetlands, a variety of nature trails, meadows, and woodland areas, each with unique features.
National Colonial Farm. With period buildings and interpretive tours, this farm provides visitors a representation of tobacco plantation life in 1775.

Be sure to visit the native tree arboretum. Prescheduled tours are available.

Ecosystem Farm. Home to a Community Supported Agriculture program, Ecosystem Farm uses the newest in sustainable agriculture technology to demonstrate that producing good, quality food can be done in harmony with nature.

Hike 6
National Colonial Farm to Oxon Hill Farm

For the first time since leaving the mouth of the Potomac at Point Lookout, the Potomac Heritage Trail enters suburbia. Still, the route does not leave the river or experience of nature behind. Thanks to early and innovative conservation efforts like Piscataway Park, the trail route is an interesting show of the urban-rural interface. Yes, there are houses and cars, but there also are significant leafy scenes and waterfront parks. And the network of conservation lands owned by the National Park Service, Maryland, and Prince George's County will take long stretches of the PHT off-road in the future. Open space along the way includes Fort Washington, Potomac Waterfront Conservation Area, Riverview Park, and stream valley parks following Piscataway and Henson creeks.

National Colonial Farm at the Accokeek Foundation

TRIP PLANNER

Start: Entrance to National Colonial Farm in Piscataway Park.
End: Oxon Cove Park.
Miles: 19
Points of Interest: Piscataway Park, Fort Washington Park, Fort Foote.
Parking: Piscataway Park, National Colonial Farm, Fort Washington
        Marina, Fort Washington Park, Fort Foote.
Water, Restrooms: Piscataway Park, National Colonial Farm,
        Fort Washington Marina, Fort Washington Park, Fort Foote,
        Oxon Hill Farm.
Provisions: Livingston Square Shopping Center.
Camping: None.

HIKE DATA

0.0   Junction of Bryan Point Road and Cactus Hill Road.
        Go east on Bryan Hill Road.
2.6   Turn left on Farmington Road.
3.1   Farmington Landing.
4.1   Turn left on Route 210.
6.2   Turn left on Old Fort Road.
8.3   Junction with Fort Washington Road at Fort Washington. Park is one
        mile west on Fort Washington Road. To continue on PHT, turn right
        and follow Fort Washington Road.
8.5   Tantallon Road. Turn left.
9.5   Arrow Park Road. Turn left
9.8   Hollybank Road. Turn left.
9.9   Swan Creek Road. Turn left.
10.7 Riverview Road. Turn right.
11.5 Keep right on Riverview Road; pass Potomac River Waterfront
        Conservation Area on left.
12.0 Riverview Park.
12.4 Junction with Henson Creek Trail.
12.5 Fort Washington Road. Turn left.
12.9 Livingston Road. Turn left.
13.0 Harmony Hall Arts and Community Center.
13.3 Piscataway House.
13.9 Oxon Hill Road. Turn left.
14.4 Fort Foote Road. Turn left.
15.6 Thornton Parkway. Keep right.
16.1 Fort Foote Historic Site.
17.3 Oxon Hill Road. Turn left.

17.5   National Harbor.

18.0   Oxon Hill Farm in Oxon Cove Park.

EXPLORING THE PHT

Piscataway Park. See Hike 5 on page 23.

Fort Washington Park. This 341-acre national park preserves a military site first constructed in 1809 and used during the War of 1812. It was rebuilt during the 19th century and was a critical part of the circle of forts protecting Washington during the Civil War. During World War I, troops mustered here in preparation for deployment in France. The fort was de-commissioned in 1939. There are picnic areas, fishing, hiking and biking trails, and a playground for children. Eagles are regular visitors, too.

Henson Creek Trail. This 5.5-mile greenway, connecting the PHT corridor with the Branch Avenue Metro, is open to bicyclists, hikers and equestrians.

Fort Foote. Fort Foote was constructed on Rozier's Bluff from 1863 to 1865 to strengthen the circle of defenses around Washington, D.C. Fort Foote was designed to protect the river entrance to the ports of Alexandria, Georgetown, and Washington. It replaced the aging Fort Washington as the primary river defense. The fort was named for Rear Admiral Andrew H. Foote, who died in 1863 from wounds received in combat the previous year. Managed by the National Park Service, the site contains the ruins of what is considered the best preserved Civil War fort in the region.

Oxon Hill Farm. The main attraction at Oxon Cove Park, this working farm interprets farm life in the early 20th century. Originally founded as a working farm for the patients of Saint Elizabeth's Hospital, the farm's barns, stable, outbuildings and farmhouse are now open to the public. Exhibits in the visitors barn display farming techniques and practices; educational programs cover such topics as animal husbandry and cropping methods.

Resources

www.southernmdisfun.com. Southern Maryland is fun! That's the moniker of a handy gateway website for traveling in PHT counties Saint Mary's and Charles, as well as in adjacent Calvert. Direct dial and internet links to each county appear below.

Charles County: www.ExploreCharlesCoMD.com

Charles County Office of Tourism: (800) 766-3386

Prince George's: www.goprincegeorgescounty.com/visitors

Prince George's Conference & Visitors Bureau: (301) 925-8300

Saint Mary's County: www.co.saint-marys.md.us/Tourism

Saint Mary's County Div. of Tourism: (800) 327-9023

Bard's Field Bed and Breakfast
Ridge, MD (301) 872-5989

Brome-Howard Inn
Saint Mary's City, MD
(301) 866-0656

Chapel Point State Park
c/o Smallwood State Park
2750 Sweden Point Road
Marbury, MD 20658
(301) 743-7613 or (800) 784-5380

Charles County Historical Society
(301) 934-8305

Fort Foote
National Capital Parks-East
National Park Service
1900 Anacostia Drive, S.E.
Washington, DC 20020
(301) 763-4600 (site manager)
www.nps.gov/fofo.html

Fort Washington
National Capital Parks-East
National Park Service
1900 Anacostia Drive, S.E.
Washington, DC 20020
(301) 763-4600 (site manager)
www.nps.gov/fowa.html

Goose Bay Marina and Campground
Welcome, MD
(301) 934-3812

Historic Saint Mary's City
P.O. Box 39
Saint Mary's City, MD 20686
(240) 895-4990
www.stmaryscity.org

La Grande RV & Camping Resort
Route 5
Leonardtown, MD
(301) 475-8550

La Plata Farmers' Market
Charles County Courthouse
(301) 934-8345 for hours and detailed directions

Mattawoman Creek Art Center
at Smallwood State Park
www.mattawomanart.org

Myrtle Grove Wildlife Management Area
www.dnr.state.md.us/publiclands/southern/myrtlegrove.asp.

National Colonial Farm
The Accokeek Foundation
3400 Bryan Point Road
Accokeek, MD 20607
(301) 283-2113
www.accokeek.org

Oxon Hill Bicycle and Trail Club
www.ohbike.org

Piscataway Park
National Capital Parks-East
National Park Service
1900 Anacostia Drive, S.E.
Washington, DC 20020
(301) 763-4600 (site manager)
www.nps.gov/pisc.html

Point Lookout State Park
P.O. Box 48
Scotland, MD 20687
(301) 872-5688
www.dnr.state.md.us/publiclands/southern/pointlookout.html

Port of Plenty B&B
8664 Port Tobacco Road
La Plata, MD 20646
(301) 934-0707

Port Tobacco Historic District
(301) 934-4313

Relax Inn
Corner of Town Square in Leonardtown
(301) 475-3011

Seaside View Campground
(301) 872-4141

Smallwood State Park
2750 Sweden Point Road
Marbury MD 20658
(301) 743-7613
www.reservations.dnr.state.md.us

Smith Island Sojourn
Ferry and visitor information:
www.smithisland.org,
(410) 425-2777

Saint Clement's Island-Potomac River Museum
38370 Point Breeze Road
Colton's Point, MD 20626
(301) 769-2222

Saint Mary's River State Park
(301) 872-5688

Saint Michael's Manor Bed and Breakfast
Scotland, MD 20687
(301) 872-4025

Hale House
Ridge, MD 20680
(301) 872-4558

Take It Easy Campground
Route 249
Callaway, MD 20620
(301) 994-0494

Thomas Stone National Historic Site
6655 Rose Hill Road
Port Tobacco, MD 20677
(301) 392-1776
www.nps.gov/thst

DISTRICT OF COLUMBIA

F ort Circle Parks, the remains of Civil War fortifications that once ringed Washington, D.C., provide an extraordinary view of the capital City. Some fortifications are managed as community parkland, others are remembered through historic sites and interpretive markers. South of the Anacostia River, parks at Fort Stanton, Fort Dupont and Fort Davis combine to create several hundred acres of parks and open space. They and other sites are connected by a trail through mature woods of poplar and oak that make it easy to forget you're walking through a major city. This is one of the routes planners are considering for the Potomac Heritage Trail in the District of Columbia.

Planners in District agencies and National Park Service offices are completing a general management plan for the Fort Circle Parks, so changes and improvements can be expected in the future. A draft of the plan, for example, suggests a new footbridge over the Anacostia River, providing direct access to Kenilworth Gardens.

West of the Anacostia, the route follows Eastern Avenue and other trails on visits to Barnard Hill Park (named for the general who supervised construction of the forts), Forts Totten, Slocum and Stevens, and enters Rock Creek Park. Combined with the wooded hikes south of the Anacostia River, trails in Rock Creek and Glover-Archbold Parks offer one of the world's premiere urban hiking experiences. All are accessible by Metrorail and Metrobus, the city's transit system.

In the city's Northwest, the route takes to the street to pass through Tenley Circle, where hikers can find food and refreshment before continuing through Glover-Archbold to the Chesapeake & Ohio Canal Towpath. From here the route follows Washington, D.C.,'s most famous trail upstream to Great Falls.

More than just fine hiking, the Washington, D.C., section of the PHT is also a great conservation story. After the Civil War, most of the 68 forts and 93 batteries were dismantled, and the land was returned to pre-war owners. Over time, remnant earthworks and fortifications were incorporated into the growing city. Before they completely disappeared, the 1902 MacMillan Plan called for purchasing key remaining sites and developing them as parkland, then creating a 23-mile parkway to connect them. This idea was the genesis of the Fort Circle Parks.

The parkway plan was abandoned in the 1960s after development along the corridor proceeded at a pace too swift to incorporate the parkway plan. Fortunately, the parkland part of the plan has resulted in a greenbelt circling the city and providing valuable open space. Today, instead of a parkway, a trail network connects many of the parks, with more connections planned.

West of the Anacostia is Rock Creek Park, one of America's oldest national parks. Its 3,200 acres offer nearly 30 miles of hiking trails and 11 miles of equestrian trails. It was established in 1890 as one of the country's first national parks, and has been integral to life in the city ever since. In the decades following the Civil War, there was an emerging realization that the United States was destined to be a great nation. A great nation needed a worthy capital city, and to be a worthy capital Washington needed a system of parks. This was a heyday for city park planning. Rock Creek Park was envisioned as much as the jewel of American urban parks as the anchor for Washington's parks.

There are two hikes in the Oxon Hill Farm to Great Falls section. The first is a long leg stretcher from to Fort DeRussey in Rock Creek Park. It is too long for most people to cover in one day, but it offers a turn-by-turn description for anyone wanting to hike the entire segment. Others can take in segments by using Metro, returning home or to a hotel room at their convenience. This hike is followed by an easy 5.6 walk from Fort DeRussey to the towpath of the Chesapeake & Ohio Canal Foundry Branch.

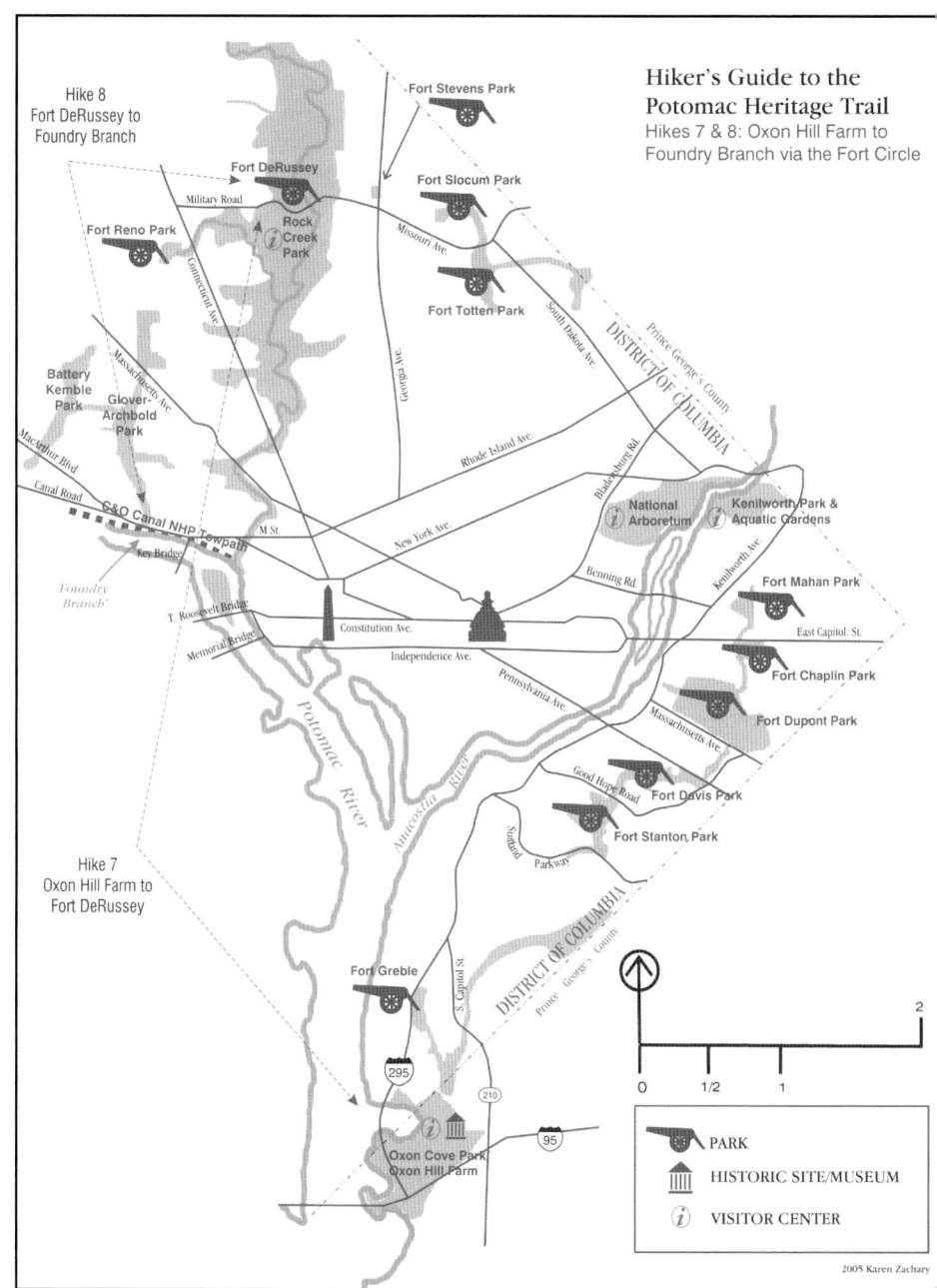

Hike 8
Fort DeRussey to
Foundry Branch

Hiker's Guide to the Potomac Heritage Trail
Hikes 7 & 8: Oxon Hill Farm to
Foundry Branch via the Fort Circle

Fort Stevens Park

Fort DeRussey

Military Road

Fort Reno Park

Rock Creek Park

Fort Slocum Park

Missouri Ave.

Connecticut Ave.

Fort Totten Park

Georgia Ave.

South Dakota Ave.

DISTRICT OF COLUMBIA

Prince George's County

Battery Kemble Park

Massachusetts Ave.

Glover-Archbold Park

Rhode Island Ave.

Bladensburg Rd.

National Arboretum

Kenilworth Park & Aquatic Gardens

MacArthur Blvd

Canal Road

C&O Canal NHP Towpath

M St.

New York Ave.

Benning Rd.

Kenilworth Ave.

Fort Mahan Park

Key Bridge

Foundry Branch

T. Roosevelt Bridge

Constitution Ave.

East Capitol. St.

Fort Chaplin Park

Memorial Bridge

Independence Ave.

Pennsylvania Ave.

Massachusetts Ave.

Fort Dupont Park

Potomac River

Anacostia River

Good Hope Road

Fort Davis Park

Hike 7
Oxon Hill Farm to
Fort DeRussey

Suitland

Parkway

Fort Stanton Park

Fort Greble

S. Capitol St.

DISTRICT OF COLUMBIA
Prince George's County

295

210

95

Oxon Cove Park
Oxon Hill Farm

0   1/2   1   2

PARK

HISTORIC SITE/MUSEUM

(i) VISITOR CENTER

2005 Karen Zachary

34

Hike 7
Along the Fort Circle Trail
Oxon Hill Farm to Fort DeRussey at Oregon Avenue

The hike begins at the Oxon Hill Farm, an historic farm at the mouth of Oxon Creek, which I-295 motorists know only as a curious green space outside their windows just before the Capital Beltway junction. They should get out of the car and check it out! Oxon Cove Park originally was conceived of as a transition zone between urban Washington and rural Prince George's County. Today it softens the transition into suburbia as it recreates an early 20th century farmstead.

Heading northeast from Oxon Hill, the route follows sidewalks to Fort Stanton Park, where it hooks up with the Fort Circle Trail.

For a truly memorable introduction to the Fort Circle hikes, consider one of the guided hikes offered by Washington Parks and People, a non-profit group that organizes volunteers and events and advocates green infrastructure for Washington, D.C. Their twice annual hikes cover the Fort Circle over a weekend. There is plenty of rest time and story-telling built into the program, along with the all-important café stops at local eateries and watering holes. Contact information for Washington Parks and People appears in the Resources section of this book.

A note about the route description that follows: Many people find it easier to navigate urban parks using street names for primary navigation. That technique is applied here. For the most part, finding your way along the adjacent trails is as easy as finding your way along the street. The exception for this hike is the stretch between Good Hope Road and Benning Road, where detailed trail descriptions are provided—you can follow the streets or the trails.

TRIP PLANNER
Start: Oxon Hill Farm.
End: Fort DeRussey in Rock Creek Park.
Miles: 19.4
Points of Interest: Oxon Hill Manor, Fort Dupont Park, Fort Slocum, Fort Stevens, Fort DeRussey.
Parking: Oxon Hill and at each fort.
Water, Restrooms: Primarily public restaurants.
Provisions: Various.
Camping: None.

HIKE DATA

0.0   Oxon Hill Farm.
0.5   Bald Eagle Drive.
0.6   Indian Head Highway. Turn left on Route 210.
1.5   Junction with Livingston Road; continue north on South Capitol Street.
1.6   Enter Washington, D.C.
1.8   Galveston Street. Turn left.
2.1   Martin L. King Jr. Avenue. Turn right.
2.2   Chesapeake Street. Turn left. Fort Greble is left one block.
2.3   Second Street. Turn right.
2.5   Atlantic Street. Turn right.
2.6   Mississippi Avenue. Turn left.
4.1   Stanton Road. Turn left.
4.6   Cross Suitland Parkway; turn right at fork.
4.7   Gainesville Road. Turn right.
4.8   16th Street. Turn left.
4.9   Erie Street. Turn right.
5.0   Fort Stanton Park. Follow the trail heading northeast through the park.
5.3   Cross Good Hope Road; enter Fort Davis Park.
5.4   Cross Naylor Road into Fort Davis Park, following trail.
5.6   28th Street. Turn left.
5.7   Turn right to enter woods.
6.1   Turn left on Park Drive and go about 100 yards. Then turn right to cross Branch Avenue and enter woods into Stanton Park.
6.5   Cross Pennsylvania Avenue; then turn left to cross Fort Davis Drive and enter woods on the path that travels between 38th Street and Fort Davis Drive.
6.9   Cross Fort Davis Drive.
7.0   Cross Massachusetts Avenue; enter Fort Dupont Park.
7.4   Cross stream on footbridge.
7.5   Stay left at junction. The trail circles a ravine providing a dramatic landscape.
7.8   Turn left at junction and continue to circle the ravine.
8.2   Pass through rhododendrons and azaleas.
8.4   Cross Fort Davis Drive.
8.9   Cross C Street and enter Fort Chapin Park.
9.1   Stay right at fork, then right at the street. Cross East Capitol Street and follow path.
9.2   Benning Road. Turn left. *[Note: If you're hiking to the Minnesota Avenue Metro stop, cross Benning Road and follow the trail to the*

right. Circle Fort Mahon on the trail, then follow 42nd Street to Lady Bird Park. Metro is one block left on Hayes.] To cross the Anacostia River, walk toward the river on Benning Road.

9.4 Cross Anacostia River on Benning Road.
10.5 Bladendsburg Road. Turn right.
12.7 Eastern Avenue at Fort Lincoln Cemetery. Turn left.
13.9 Varnum Street. Turn left.
14.0 Gallatin Street. Turn right.
15.1 South Dakota Street. Turn right.
15.2 Galloway Street. Turn left.
15.4 Cross under railroad tracks into Fort Totten Park on 1st Place. Follow 1st Place to Riggs Road.
15.6 Riggs Road. Turn left.
15.7 1st Place. Turn right. Trails are planned along this greenway.
15.9 McDonald Place. Turn left.
16.1 Blair Road. Turn right.
16.2 At Oglethorpe Street (on right), turn left and cross through park.
16.3 Cross Kansas Avenue in Fort Slocum Park. Follow footpath northwest through park toward Oglethorpe Street.
16.5 Oglethorpe Street. Turn left.
17.0 7th Street. Turn right.
17.1 Quackenbos Street. Turn left.
17.4 Cross Georgia Avenue.
17.5 Fort Stevens Park. Pass through into west side of park.
17.6 Follow Fort Stevens Road.
17.9 16th Street. Turn right.
18.0 Joyce Road at intersection with Rittenhouse Street. Turn left.
18.4 Cross Military Road.
18.8 Junction with Valley Trail. Cross Rock Creek.
18.9 Fort DeRussey Trail. Turn right.
19.1 Fort DeRussey. Continue on path to Oregon Avenue.
19.4 Oregon Avenue, parking.

EXPLORING THE PHT
Oxon Cove Park. See Hike 6 on page 25.
Fort Dupont. This 376-acre park is one of the largest in the city. The fort had six sides, each 100 feet long, and was surrounded by a deep moat. It was named for Flag Officer Samuel F. Dupont, who commanded the naval victory at Port Royal, South Carolina, in November 1861. The only traces of the fort today are the earthworks that can be traced near the picnic area. During the Civil War, the siege guns of Fort Dupont guarded the Eleventh Street bridge over the Anacostia River near the Washington Navy

Yard. Although the troops here never saw battle, Fort Dupont was a welcoming harbor for runaway slaves. The National Capital Planning Commission acquired the old fort and surrounding land for recreation in the 1930s. A popular mountain biking spot, the site houses an activity center that offers programs and restrooms.

Fort Slocum. Fort Slocum was built by the Second Rhode Island Infantry and named for its commander, Colonel John S. Slocum, who was killed at the First Battle of Bull Run. Today it is a peaceful, wooded park. It's a terrific spot for a rest stop on the PHT. Fort Slocum had 25 guns and mortars and commanded the intersection of the left and right forks of Rock Creek Church Road (near today's New Hampshire Avenue and McDonald Place). The field gun battery and rifle-pits are badly eroded, but remain visible in Fort Slocum Park, bounded by Kansas Avenue, Blair Road, and Milmarson Place, NE.

Photo by Paul g. Wiegman

Fort Stevens. General Jubal Early attacked Fort Stevens July 11-12, 1864, marking two unique moments in history. It was the only attack directly on Washington, D.C. during the Civil War. It also is the only time a sitting U.S. President was present in battle. The President and Mrs. Lincoln came out from the city to observe the battle. With support from Forts DeRussey and Slocum, and from reinforcements rushed to the scene, the attack was repulsed. The fort is partially restored, making it possible to visualize the way it looked in the 1860s. There are no visitor facilities available, but there are plenty of eateries on nearby Georgia Avenue.

Fort DeRussey. Fort DeRussy was built on a hill to provide cross fire on the approaches to Fort Stevens on the 7th Street Pike (now Georgia Avenue) and to control the countryside to west of today's Rock Creek Park. It supported Fort Stevens in the only battle fought in Washington, D.C. during the Civil War, July 11-12, 1864. It was built in 1861 by the Fourth New York Heavy Artillery and named after its commander, Colonel Gustavus A. DeRussy. Relatively well-preserved, the parapet's earthworks still display the openings where guns were mounted. The moat around the parapet is evident, and rifle trenches outside the parapet can be seen.

Hike 8
Along the Fort Circle and Glover-Archbold Trails
Fort DeRussey to the Chesapeake & Ohio Canal Towpath

Perhaps what's most amazing about this stroll down tree-line sidewalks and wooded paths is how few people know it exists. On this hike you can experience Washington, D.C. neighborhoods, a few sites along the Fort Circle Parks Trail and one of the area's best-kept secrets—Foundry Branch Trail in Glover-Archbold Park.

Best of all, you can be sitting at home on a weekend morning, decide to take this hike, and be out on the trail in no time at all. There's no need to pack a lunch because the midpoint of the segment goes right through Tenley Circle. Both ends are accessible via public transportation. You can also do just the north or south portions, using the Metro station at Tenley as an end point.

TRIP PLANNER
Start: Oregon Avenue at Fort Russey in Rock Creek Park.
End: Chesapeake & Ohio National Historical Park at Canal Road and Foundry Branch.
Miles: 5.6
Points of Interest: Fort DeRussey.
Parking: Oregon Ave., near Fort DeRussey (0.0), Fort Reno on Chesapeake Street. (2.0), Canal Road (5.6).
Water, Restrooms: Tenley Circle restaurants.
Provisions: Tenley Circle stores and restaurants.
Camping: None.

HIKE DATA
0.0   From Oregon Avenue entrance to Rock Creek Park, go south on the Western Ridge Trail.
0.1   Military Road.
0.4   Grant Road. Turn right.

0.6	Broad Branch Road. Turn right.
1.2	36th Street. Turn left
1.5	Cross Connecticut Avenue.
1.6	Turn right on Ellicott Street.
1.7	Reno Road. Turn left, then immediately right on Fort Drive.
1.8	Cross Nebraska Avenue.
1.9	Fort Reno Park.
2.0	Chesapeake Street, at south end of park. Go south on 40th Street away from park.
2.3	Cross Tenley Circle; stay on 40th Street.
2.4	Veasy Street. Turn right, then left at the end of the street.
2.5	Van Ness Street. Turn left.
2.6	Turn right on foot trail into Glover-Archbold Park.
3.3	Cross Massachusetts Avenue.
3.7	Cross Cathedral Avenue.
3.9	Cross New Mexico Avenue.
4.1	Reach footpath to Battery Kemble and Palisades Park— planned future route for PHT. To continue on PHT, continue south. (For a side trip to Battery Kemble, turn right here, then turn right at the trail fork. Cross 44th Street at Edmonds Street; then stay on the trail. Cross Foxhall Road. Cross 49th Street into Palisades Park.)
4.4	Trail junction. Continue straight.
4.8	Trail junction. The path leads left (east) into Whitehaven Park.
5.1	Cross Reservoir Road.
5.6	Tunnel under MacArthur Boulevard. Reach C&O Canal Towpath at Canal Road and Foundry Branch.

EXPLORING THE PHT
Fort DeRussey. See Hike 7 on page 35.

Fort Reno. Originally named Fort Pennsylvania for the 119th Pennsylvania Regiment which constructed it, the fort was renamed for Major General Jesse Lee Reno, who died from wounds received at the Battle of South Mountain in 1862. It was built during the winter of 1861 shortly after the Union Army's defeat at the First Battle of Manassas. Situated at the highest point in Washington, Fort Reno eventually became the largest and most heavily-armed fort circling the city. Its commanding views of the surrounding countryside made it an important link in the defense of Washington. Today, in addition to serving as parkland, the Fort Reno site contains reservoirs for Washington's drinking water.

Glover-Archbold Park. A three-mile trail runs the length of the park, which stretches from the Potomac River nearly to Tenley Circle. With seven stream crossings along the way, the defining feature of the route is

Foundry Branch. For a 3.5-mile circuit hike, begin at Tenley Circle and hike south into Glover-Archbold (at mile 2.3 above). Turn right at the trail to Battery Kemble (mile 4.1). Once in Battery Kemble, turn right and follow the trail to Nebraska Avenue; then follow Nebraska back to Tenley Circle. **Battery Kemble.** People who grow up in Washington, D.C., know Battery Kemble Park as one the best sledding hills in the city. During the Civil War it was one of 93 batteries supporting the 68 forts defending the city. A potential future route for the Potomac Heritage National Scenic Trail leads to Battery Kemble then south to the C&O Canal Towpath.

RESOURCES
C&O Canal
www.nps.gov/choh/

DC Heritage Tourism Coalition
www.culturaltourismdc.org

Fort Dupont Recreation Center
www.nps.gov/fodu

Kenilworth Park and Aquatic Gardens
www.cr.nps.gov/museum/collections/keaq.html

NPS National Capital-East
(202) 690-5185
www.nps.gov/nace

NPS National Capital-Central
(202) 426-6841
www.nps.gov/nacc

U.S. National Arboretum
www.usna.usda.gov

Rock Creek Park
www.nps.gov/rocr

Washington Parks and People
www.washingtonparks.net

UP THE C&O TO HARPERS FERRY

The hikes in this section follow the towpath of the Chesapeake & Ohio Canal National Historical Park. The 184.5-mile linear park preserves and interprets the role of canals in America's westward expansion. Work began in 1828 with the goal of connecting Georgetown and the Forks of the Ohio in Pittsburgh. Obsolete before it was finished in 1850, the canal nonetheless played an important role the nation's history and operated sporadically until 1924.

Nearly as amazing as the task of building the canal is the success in preserving it. In the 1950s a planned parkway running the length of the C&O Canal had wide public support. Yet, somehow a band of caring citizens made the case to save it. The help they received from Supreme Court Justice William O. Douglas is now itself part of conservation history.

Had the highway been built, surely the landscape along the Potomac would be dramatically different today. And had the effort to preserve the canal come only 20 years later, it would have been hard-pressed to keep ahead of the rapid growth the region has undergone.

Among the many sites visited by the towpath is Glen Echo Park, begun in 1891 as a National Chautauqua Assembly, an education organization whose mission was to prepare people for citizenship and inspire an appreciation of the arts and literature. After the Chautauqua faded, Glen Echo became a popular amusement park, operating until 1968. Today the reborn park offers arts education programs, performances and concerts.

This segment also passes Clara Barton National Historic Site, early headquarters of the American Red Cross and home to its founder Clara Barton. The formation of the Red Cross marks an important chapter in American history as one of the first international efforts in which the U.S. became deeply involved.

Decades before the C&O Canal Park was created, hikers appreciated the natural beauty of the narrow greenway created by the canal. As the City of Washington has grown into a major metropolis, the canal corridor has become an even greater environmental resource. Few of the world's major rivers are followed so closely over so many miles by a greenway. Few rivers have so many access points for putting in and taking out.

On this section, the towpath climbs from tidewater through the Piedmont and into the northern Blue Ridge at Harpers Ferry, West Virginia. This section also marks the third historical period explored by a PHT segment on this side of the river. The first period traces early settlement in the lower Potomac; the second follows the Civil War in Washington, D.C. In the Piedmont, the towpath tells the story of the agrarian small-town era in which the rural economy was linked to Washington—culturally a world away.

The final miles of the segment leave the Piedmont to travel within the Catoctin and Blue Ridge Mountains. The terrain surrounding the trail is rugged and dramatic, and the history is linked to minerals and early manufacturing. The wooded slopes seen today are second and third growth forests. The first wave of cutting leveled entire mountainsides to fuel coke furnaces that provided fuel for nearby mills and munitions plants in Harpers Ferry. Later, recovering woods were thinned and cleared for pasture, as the middle Potomac was transformed into the region's dairyland.

Of all the forces of change affecting both sides of the river from the Route 15 crossing near Point of Rocks to Harpers Ferry, perhaps none has been as powerful as the opening of Dulles International Airport in 1962. The airport and the emergence of Washington, D.C. as a major metropolis put in motion a transition to suburbia that continues today.

Note: For hikes along the towpath in this guidebook, mileages relate to number of miles in each particular hike; they do not correspond with the mile markers on the towpath.

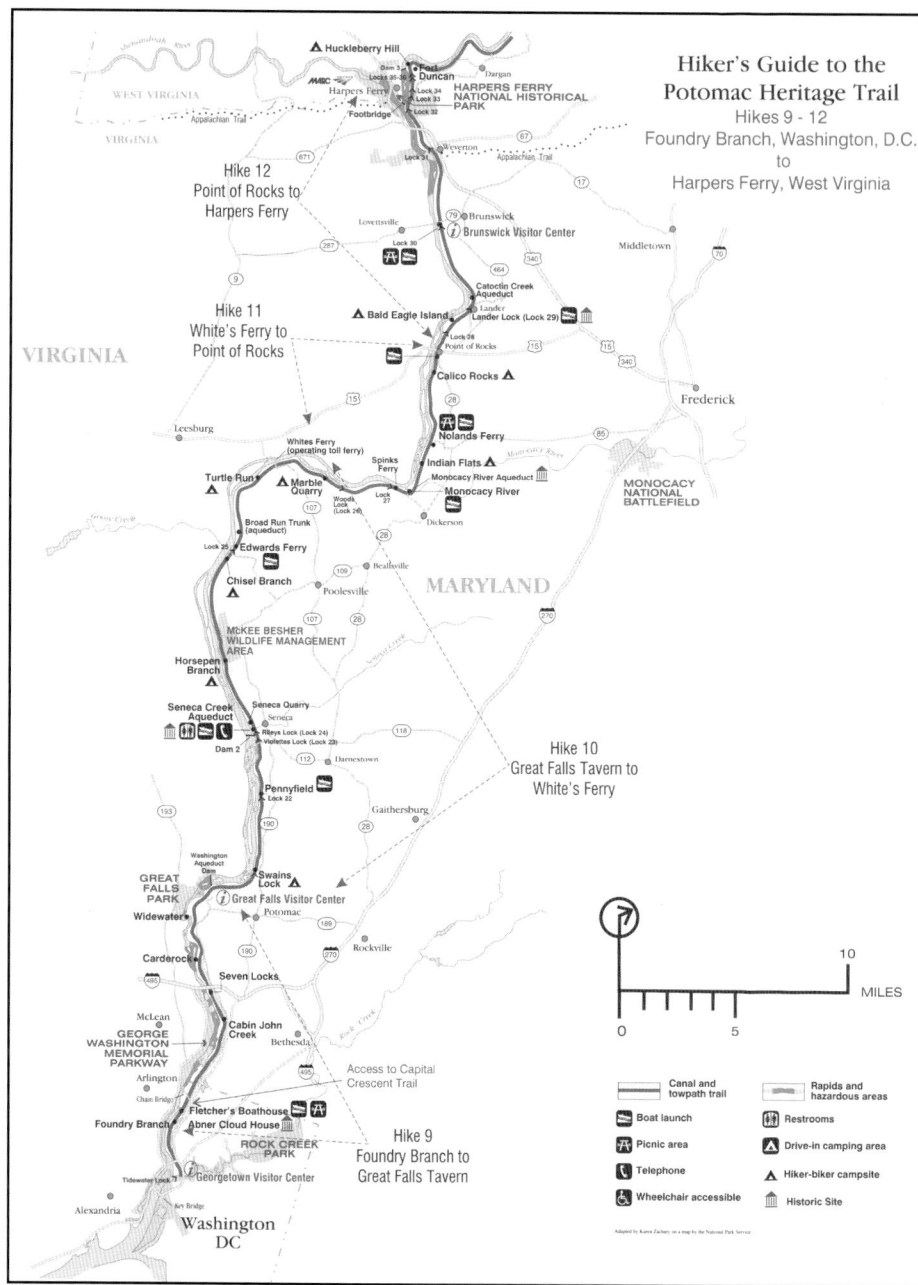

Hiker's Guide to the
Potomac Heritage Trail
Hikes 9 - 12
Foundry Branch, Washington, D.C.
to
Harpers Ferry, West Virginia

WEST VIRGINIA

VIRGINIA

▲ Huckleberry Hill

Ford
Duncan
Dargan
HARPERS FERRY
NATIONAL HISTORICAL
PARK
Harpers Ferry
Footbridge
Weverton
Appalachian Trail

Hike 12
Point of Rocks to
Harpers Ferry

Brunswick
Brunswick Visitor Center
Lock 30

Middletown

Catoctin Creek
Aqueduct

Hike 11
White's Ferry to
Point of Rocks

VIRGINIA

▲ Bald Eagle Island
Lander Lock (Lock 29)
Point of Rocks

Calico Rocks ▲

Leesburg

Frederick

Nolands Ferry

Turtle Run
▲

Whites Ferry
(operating toll ferry)
Spinks
Ferry
Indian Flats ▲

Marble
Quarry
Monocacy River Aqueduct
Monocacy River

MONOCACY
NATIONAL
BATTLEFIELD

Broad Run Trunk
(aqueduct)

Woods
Lock
(Lock 26)
Lock
27

Dickerson

Lock 25
Edwards Ferry

Chisel Branch
▲

Beallsville

Poolesville

MARYLAND

McKEE BESHER
WILDLIFE MANAGEMENT
AREA

Horsepen
Branch
▲

Seneca Creek
Aqueduct
Dam 2

Seneca Quarry
Seneca
Rileys Lock (Lock 24)
Violettes Lock (Lock 23)

Darnestown

Hike 10
Great Falls Tavern to
White's Ferry

Pennyfield
Lock 22

Gaithersburg

Washington
Aqueduct
Dam

Swains
Lock ▲

GREAT
FALLS
PARK

Great Falls Visitor Center
Potomac

Widewater

Rockville

Carderock

Seven Locks

McLean
GEORGE
WASHINGTON
MEMORIAL
PARKWAY

Cabin John
Creek
Bethesda

Arlington

Chain Bridge

Access to Capital
Crescent Trail

Fletcher's Boathouse
Abner Cloud House

Foundry Branch

ROCK CREEK
PARK

Hike 9
Foundry Branch to
Great Falls Tavern

Tidewater Lock
Georgetown Visitor Center

Alexandria

Key Bridge

Washington
DC

10
MILES
0   5

Canal and
towpath trail

Rapids and
hazardous areas

Boat launch

Restrooms

Picnic area

Drive-in camping area

Telephone

Hiker-biker campsite

Wheelchair accessible

Historic Site

44

Hike 9
Along the C&O Canal
Foundry Branch to Great Falls Tavern

The original plan for the C&O Canal was to connect the tidewater Potomac with the Ohio River. Financial problems, floods and railroad competition combined to stall the idea at Cumberland, Maryland. The canal operated until 1924 when a spring flood closed the route for the last time. It became the property of the federal government in 1938 and a national park in 1971. It is by far the best preserved of the early American canals.

Sixteen locks and five lock houses make this area one of the best places to get a sense of canal life. Widewater and Great Falls highlight the tremendous obstacles that had to be overcome to build the canal. As you notice the bands of rock along the canal berm, remember each had to be blasted with black powder, then removed by hand. At Widewater, a natural channel of the Potomac River allows for a spectacular approach to Great Falls. Accompanied by the roar of the falls, your journey ends at the restored Great Falls Tavern, which was built in 1831 and now houses a small museum and visitor center.

TRIP PLANNER

Start: Foundry Branch.

End: Great Falls Tavern.

Miles: 12.8

Points of Interest: Fletcher's Boathouse; Abner Cloud House; B&O Railroad trestle; Guard Lock 1; Seven Locks; Widewater; Great Falls, Great Falls Tavern.

Parking: Fletcher's Boathouse (1.6 mi.); Chain Bridge (2.7 mi.); Lock 5 (3.5 mi.); Lock 6 (3.9 mi.); Lock 7 (5.5 mi.); Cabin John Bridge (6.0 mi.); Lock 8 (6.8 mi.); Lock 10 (7.3 mi.); Carderock Recreation Area (8.9 mi.); Widewater (10.8 mi.); Great Falls (12.8 mi.).

Water: Fletcher's; Lock 5; Carderock; Great Falls.

Restroom or Privy: Fletcher's; Lock 5; Carderock; Great Falls.

Provisions: Fletcher's, limited snacks, April through November; Great Falls, snack bar in season.

Camping: Marsden Tract, groups only, permit needed.

HIKE DATA

0.0 Foundry Branch. The trail passes under the canal. Turn left and climb steps to the towpath. Turn left again to head west.

1.6 Fletcher's Boathouse. Snacks, boat and bike rentals are available, April through November.

1.6 Abner Cloud House, oldest structure on canal, stands across from Fletcher's on the berm.

2.1 B&O Railroad trestle. Stairs here provide access to Capital Crescent Trail (CCT). The CCT leads three miles back to Georgetown. Or you could turn right and cross the trestle to follow the CCT 7.5 miles to Bethesda. This trestle and the tunnel to the north were built in 1910.

2.7 Chain Bridge. Access to the PHT in Virginia is across the river.

3.5 Lock 5 and Guard Lock 1.

3.9 Lock 6. The lock house here is one of the few on the canal in which people still live.

4.1 Little Falls Skirting Canal. Near this spot on July 4, 1828, President John Quincy Adams broke ground for the canal. That same day in Baltimore a separate groundbreaking took place for the B&O Railroad.

5.5 Lock 7.

6.0 Cabin John Bridge. When completed in 1864, this was the longest stone-arch bridge in the world.

6.8 Lock 8.

7.3 Lock 10.

8.9 Carderock Recreation Area. Water is available here.

10.0 Marsden Tract. Group camping is available by reservation.

10.8 Widewater. Bicycles should detour to the Berm Road in order to avoid a rugged section of towpath. The Berm Road route rejoins towpath at the stop lock by the entrance to the Billy Goat Trail.

12.3 Billy Goat Trail. Constructed by the Red Triangle Hiking Club in 1919, this is a rugged two-mile path requiring sturdy footwear.

12.6 Olmstead Island Trail. Boardwalk and bridges lead 0.2 miles to overlook of Great Falls.

12.8 Great Falls Tavern. During the spring and summer a snack bar operates just to the west of the tavern and canal boat rides leave from the lock. The restored lockhouse features a museum.

EXPLORING THE PHT

Fletcher's Boathouse. There is something for everyone here. Canoes, rowboats and bicycles can be rented. There is access to the Potomac River and the popular Capital Crescent Trail (CCT). A bridge from the parking lot connects to a ramp which allows access to the CCT for wheelchair users. A snack bar, plenty of shade trees and picnic tables allow for leisure. The Abner Cloud House, the oldest structure along the C&O, sits just across the canal.

Widewater. This unique area is really a river channel, with towering cliffs and dark forests above. The towpath follows a rugged route on a levee. The Berm Road traces a high route on the north or berm side (the side opposite the river). This is a dark shaded route. You are actually walking on the 12-mile Washington Aqueduct built by the Army Corps of Engineers in 1853. The towpath can be combined with the Billy Goat Trail to form a loop. This rugged trail follows cliff tops on Bear Island past enormous boulders.

Great Falls. You visit the falls by strolling across boardwalks and bridges to Olmstead Island. The old tavern is now a museum featuring two films about the canal. One is a silent film from 1916 and remains the only known film of the canal in operation. The other was filmed for the American Bicentennial celebration. During spring and summer, a barge ride is offered which features passage through Lock 20 in front of the tavern. Behind the lockhouse a series of trails leads to a goldmine ruin and along a historic trolley line. These trails also link to the Berm Road, making yet another loop possible.

Hike 10
Along the C&O Canal
Great Falls Tavern to Whites Ferry

Above Great Falls, the canal takes on more of a rural feel. Soon Swains Lock comes into view. From downstream it appears as it did in the 1830s. Moving ahead, dramatic cliffs topped with cedars and a river filled with islands grace the route. To provide a foundation for the towpath, a two-mile long rock wall was built between Swains and Pennyfield Lock. Eventually, the cliffs fall away and the canal climbs to Seneca Aqueduct. West of Seneca Creek the route changes character. The canal here is filled with large trees. The towpath narrows and gets rougher. On most days, from here to Cumberland you will see only a handful of people. Past Edwards Ferry, turf farms and grazing lands of Montgomery County's Agricultural Reserve line the trail.

The trail emerges from the woods at Whites Ferry. Nearly 100 ferries have operated on the Potomac over the last 175 years. Now there is only one. You have to ride it. If you're traveling by car, take a short trip to Leesburg. You can cycle into Leesburg, then head home on the Washington & Old Dominion Trail. Or just ride to the other side and back.

TRIP PLANNER

Start: Great Falls Tavern.
End: Whites Ferry.
Miles: 21.5
Points of Interest: Great Falls Tavern and Museum; Swains Lock, Seneca Creek Aqueduct; Edwards Ferry; Broad Run Aqueduct; Whites Ferry.
Parking: Great Falls (0.0 mi.); Swains Lock (2.3 mi.); Pennyfield Lock (5.3 mi.); Violettes Lock (7.8 mi.); Seneca Creek Aqueduct (8.5 mi.); Sycamore Landing (12.9 mi.); Edwards Ferry (16.6); Whites Ferry (21.5 mi.).
Water: Great Falls; Swains Lock; Seneca Aqueduct; and Horsepen Branch, Chisel Branch, and Turtle Run campsites (water is typically turned off November through March).
Restroom or Privy: Great Falls; Swains Lock; Seneca Creek Aqueduct; Horsepen Branch Campsite; Chisel Branch Campsite; Turtle Run Campsite; Whites Ferry.
Provisions: Great Falls, snack bar in season; Seneca Aqueduct; groceries 0.9 miles up Riley's Lock Road (closed on Sunday); Whites Ferry (limited groceries and snack bar in season).
Campsites: Swains Lock; Horsepen Branch; Chisel Branch; Turtle Run.

HIKE DATA

0.0   Great Falls Tavern. During spring and summer a snack bar operates near the tavern. Canal boat rides leave from the lock. The restored lock house features a museum.

2.3   Swains Lock. The Swain family was operating this lock when the canal closed in 1924. Swain family descendents still live in the lockhouse. Snacks are sold here April through October. There are boats and bicycles for rent.

5.3   Pennyfield Lock. The ruined house on the berm was owned by the Pennyfields. President Grover Cleveland stayed here when fishing in the area.

7.8   Violettes Lock.

8.4   Seneca Creek Aqueduct. Lockhouse tours by chance on Saturdays. Poole's General Store is 0.9 miles to the right. To reach it, follow the road along creek to River Road, then turn left and cross bridge to store.

11.7 Horsepen Branch Campsite. This is the first of the regular hiker-biker campsites.

12.9 Sycamore Landing.

16.1 Chisel Branch Campsite.

16.6 Edwards Ferry. The ruins here are the remains of Jarboe's Store.

17.7 Broad Run Aqueduct, the only wooden aqueduct of 12 aqueducts on the C&O. The wooden flume is gone but the stone supports have been restored.

20.2 Turtle Run Campsite.

21.5 Whites Ferry. This is the last operating ferry on the Potomac. A snack bar operates here April through October. Sodas are available from the vending machines outside. Passage on the ferry is 50 cents for pedestrians; bicycles are $1.00. There are canoes and Johnboats for rent; and float trips are offered.

EXPLORING THE PHT
Great Falls. See Hike 9 on page 45.

Seneca Creek. The red sandstone quarried in the vicinity was used to be build the Seneca Creek Aqueduct and the Smithsonian Castle in Washington. Just west of the aqueduct, at the junction with the Seneca Greenway, stands the ruins of the Seneca Stone Cutting Mill. The location also marks the beginning of the Seneca Greenway, a trail that meanders up the creek and cross-county, eventually reaching the Patuxent River.

Whites Ferry. Ferrying across a river is becoming an increasingly rare experience. Spend a dollar on a round trip on the Potomac River, and step back into time.

Lift Locks. Canal locks are used to raise or lower canal water to meet the surrounding terrain. This enables the boats to float on flat water. On the C&O Canal, a boat would enter a chamber between a set of gates. If the boat was traveling upstream, the chamber filled with water, lifting the boat. Then the upper gate would open, allowing the boat to pass through. For a boat headed downstream, the lock would be full of water when the boat entered. The lower gate would then be opened, draining water from the lock and lowering the boat so it could proceed downstream. The C&O Canal had 74 lift locks. Each lifted boats an average of eight feet, for a total elevation change of 605 feet from Cumberland and Georgetown.

Hike 11
Along the C&O Canal
Whites Ferry to Point of Rocks

Along the towpath in this section there are enormous sycamore trees, recognized by their peeling bark. They take on a whitish color in winter. Woods Lock, just past milepost 39, sits in a beautiful remote setting. Once the railroad joins on the berm side, it is a frequent neighbor all the way to Cumberland. The segment ends at Point of Rocks, where the towpath is tucked under the towering cliffs of the Catoctin Mountains.

TRIP PLANNER
Start: Whites Ferry.

End: Point of Rocks.

Miles: 12.4

Points of Interest: Whites Ferry; Dickerson; Monocacy Aqueduct; Point of Rocks.

Parking: Whites Ferry (0.0 mi.); Dickerson (3.9 mi.); Monocacy Aqueduct (6.4 mi.); Nolands Ferry (8.8 mi.); Point of Rocks (12.4 mi.).

Water: Marble Quarry Campsite; Indian Flats Campsite; Calico Rocks Campsite; Point of Rocks. The water pumps at C&O campsites typically are inoperable November through April.

Restroom or Privy: Whites Ferry; Marble Quarry Campsite; Indian Flats; Nolands Ferry; Calico Rocks Campsite.

Provisions: Whites Ferry, limited groceries and snack bar in season; Point of Rocks, limited groceries are available at the deli on Route 28—check out daily breakfast and lunch specials.

Camping: Marble Quarry Campsite; Indian Flats Campsite; Calico Rocks Campsite.

HIKE DATA
0.0 Whites Ferry. This is the last operating ferry on the Potomac River. A snack bar operates here April through October. Sodas are available from the vending machine outside.

2.4 Marble Quarry Campsite.

3.6 Woods Lock.

3.9 Dickerson. The canal has been re-watered here, creating a popular fishing spot.

6.4 Monocacy Aqueduct. At 516 feet long, it is the longest aqueduct on the canal.

6.6 Indian Flats Campsite.

8.8 Nolands Ferry. Martha Washington is said to have crossed here to visit General George Washington at Valley Forge.

11.8 Calico Rocks Campsite.

12.4 Point of Rocks. There is a small store and deli located on the main street about 300 yards from the towpath; follow boat access road to Route 28. The town is served by MARC trains weekdays.

EXPLORING THE PHT
Whites Ferry. See Hike 10 on page 47.

Monocacy Aqueduct. Aqueducts were structures that served as water bridges to carry the canal across rivers and creeks. There were 12 aqueducts on the C&O, 11 built of stone and one of wood. Completed in

1833, the Monocacy Aqueduct is widely considered the most magnificent structure on the canal. It had been severely damaged in 1972 by Hurricane Agnes, and for more than 30 years was held together by braces. After extensive restoration, it has been returned to its full former glory. Instead of water and canal boats, it now carries the towpath's visitors across the Monocacy. Fishing and paddling are popular here.

Point of Rocks. Efforts to extend the canal and railroad west came to a grinding halt here. The railroad and canal companies both claimed ownership of the narrow passage between the rocks and river. A legal battle ensued that delayed construction for years. After losing the court battle, the B&O built a tunnel here in 1868. Point of Rocks features a railroad station, built in 1871, that is listed on the National Register of Historic Places. This is the first of three towns along the canal (along with Brunswick and Harpers Ferry) that are served by MARC commuter trains on weekdays, making it possible to hike out of town on the weekend and head back in for work on Monday morning.

Hike 12
Along the C&O Canal
Point of Rocks to Harpers Ferry

At Point of Rocks, the towpath cuts through the Catoctin Mountains. On the other side of the mountain, the trail crosses a "Bailey Bridge," installed when the Catoctin Aqueduct collapsed in 1973. Bailey Bridges, designed by a British engineer in the latter stages of World War II, are prefabricated structures assembled on site.

Eight miles west of Point of Rocks, the towpath comes to the railroad town of Brunswick—at one time the nation's largest railroad yard. At Weverton, the trail is joined from the north by the Appalachian National Scenic Trail. The trails co-align for 2.6 miles into Harpers Ferry. The hike ends under the railroad trestle at Harpers Ferry.

TRIP PLANNER
Start: Point of Rocks.
End: Harpers Ferry.
Miles: 12.5
Points of Interest: Lander Lockhouse; Brunswick; Appalachian Trail; Harpers Ferry.
Parking: Point of Rocks (0.0 mi.); Lock 29 (2.7 mi.); Brunswick (6.8 mi.).
Water: Point of Rocks; Bald Eagle Island Campsite; Brunswick Campground; Brunswick; Harpers Ferry; (water at campsites normally turned off November through April).
Restroom or Privy: Bald Eagle Island Campsite; Brunswick Campground; Harpers Ferry.
Provisions: Point of Rocks; Brunswick; Harpers Ferry.
Camping: Bald Eagle Island campsite; Brunswick Campground.

HIKE DATA
0.0   Point of Rocks. There is a small store and deli located on the main street about 300 yards from the towpath; follow boat access road to Route 28. The town is served by MARC trains weekdays.
1.1   Bald Eagle Island Campsite.
2.7   Lander Lockhouse. The lockhouse here has been fully restored by a volunteer organization. Tours are given on weekends in summer.
3.3   Catoctin Aqueduct. This aqueduct was known as the "Crooked Aqueduct" because of sharp turn at west end. It collapsed in 1973 and has been replaced by a "Bailey Bridge."
5.8   Brunswick Municipal campground. Services include water and sodas along with campsites, fee charged. Proceed with caution: slow moving car traffic on the towpath for next mile to Brunswick.

6.8   Brunswick, Md.

9.9   Appalachian Trail (AT) coming from Maine joins the towpath from the north. From here to the trestle at Harpers Ferry the routes are co-aligned.

11.4   Sandy Hook Bridge. This bridge carried the AT across the Potomac from 1948 - 1985.

12.5   Harpers Ferry. You can reach town by climbing the spiral staircase to the walkway that carries the AT across the Potomac River. From Harpers Ferry, the AT heads south to Georgia. Harpers Ferry National Historical Park features restored buildings, exhibits, a visitor center and bookstore. Restrooms and water are available during park hours.

EXPLORING THE PHT
Point of Rocks. See Hike 11 on page 49.

Brunswick. This is a quintessential railroad town. Stop at the restored depot or visit the Brunswick Railroad Museum and Canal Visitor Center on Potomac Street. Book Crossing, a block from the depot, serves coffee and sells magazines, as well as books on local history. Beans in the Belfry, a couple blocks up Potomac Street, is a funky cafe in a former church building; it serves up organic coffees, wraps and sandwiches. King's Pizza bakes a fine spinach pie.

Appalachian Trail. This is your chance to take a hike on this world famous trail. To the north, just over a mile away is Weverton Cliffs. The views from here are well worth the climb. To follow the trail turn right (north) just beyond Lock 31 and follow the white blazes. At Harpers Ferry, the AT crosses the bridge into town, crosses the Shenandoah and ascends to Loudoun Heights in Virginia.

Harpers Ferry. This historic town has been restored by the National Park Service. Exhibits interpret 19th century life in a manufacturing town, abolitionists John Brown's raid on the federal armory, and Civil War history. The famous "Bloody Stone Steps," which reportedly ran with blood during an 1862 battle, climb a short distance to Jefferson Rock. Near this spot the states of Maryland, Virginia and West Virginia meet. In his Notes on the State of Virginia, Thomas Jefferson wrote that the view here was "worth a voyage across the Atlantic."

The town features antique shops, B&Bs, restaurants and, a block up Washington Street, an outfitter. Harpers Ferry is served by both MARC and Amtrak. In addition to the C&O, the town features two other canals: the Shenandoah Navigation on Virginius Island and the Armory Canal along the Potomac upstream from the train station. Both date to the early 1800s and feature interesting ruins. Maryland Heights features numerous Civil War trenches and structures which can be seen from a trail that circles above the town. Harpers Ferry also is the home of the Appalachian Trail Conservancy (ATC).

RESOURCES

Amtrak
(800) 872-7245
www.amtrak.com

Appalachian Trail Conservancy
(304) 535-6331
www.appalachiantrail.org

Harpers Ferry NHP
www.nps.gov/hafe

Chesapeake & Ohio Canal National Historic Park
www.nps.gov/choh/

Great Falls Tavern
(301) 299-3613

MARC (Commuter Train)
(800) 325-7245
www.mtamaryland.com/

Poole's Store
(301) 948-5372

Swains Lock
(301) 299-9006

Whites Ferry
(301) 349-5200

HARPERS FERRY, W.VA.
TO CUMBERLAND, MD.

Harpers Ferry National Historical Park's exhibits and museums tell the story of a remote factory town in the nineteenth century. It was a different kind of rural life than the pastoral agricultural communities of the Piedmont and the tobacco and shellfish economy of the lower river. Here the nineteenth century's "new economy" was based on extracting raw materials from the earth and manufacturing them into finished goods to be sold and used somewhere else.

Downstream, history is seen in the open land and water. There are remnant cement kilns that served canal builders, faint traces of charcoal pits where the surrounding forests were turned into fuel for factories, and the remains of small rubble dams that created enough slackwater to move small boats upriver.

En route to Hancock, the Great Valley and the mountains west of the Blue Ridge were America's apple basket for decades. Dairy cows were ubiquitous in bottom land until the late twentieth century. Apples continue to be a leading agricultural product—despite successful marketing programs that promote the big and shiny apples of the Northwest over the smaller, delectably delicious apples of the Potomac. But the orchards are disappearing over time.

The Potomac River here flows through the Valley and Ridge province, marked by long, narrow ridges rising above the wide Great Valley that stretches from the lower Appalachians to New England. More than typography, this section offers a hiking experience that is different than the southerly segments of the towpath. Here, the skies are darker at night, there are fewer encounters with other hikers, and the wildlife is more abundant. And the river seems just a bit wilder. With the exception of a section south of Hancock, where Interstate 70 is a close companion, this section offers quiet hikes that make for fine backpacking.

The route passes Fort Frederick, a fine spot to camp after an afternoon paddle, and Green Ridge State Forest, which has plenty of room for a backpacking trip.

In this section, the towpath also visits small towns that grew up along the canal and railroad. So while you can enjoy solitude by day, you can also get supper and a bed at night.

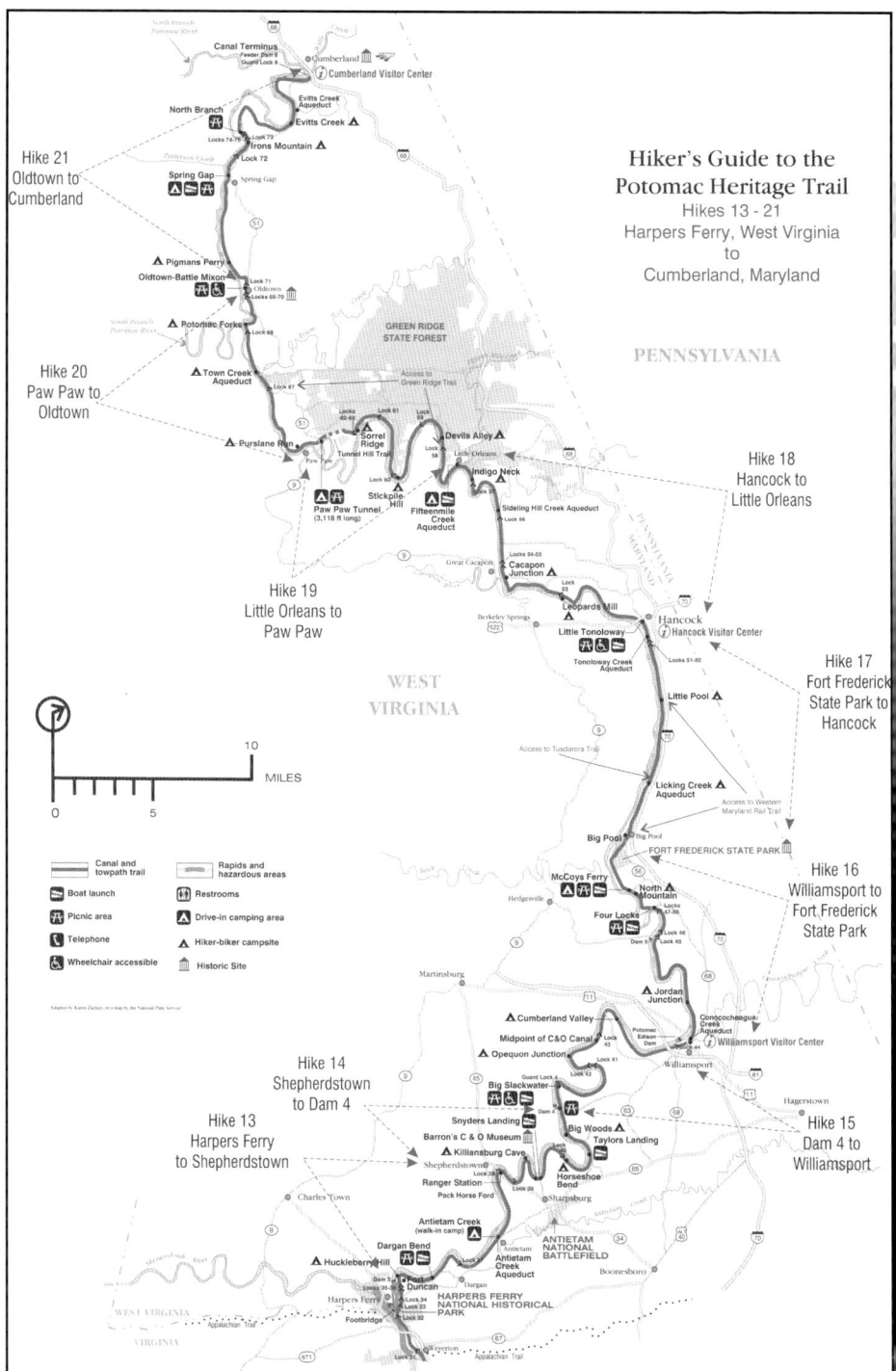

Hiker's Guide to the
Potomac Heritage Trail
Hikes 13 - 21
Harpers Ferry, West Virginia
to
Cumberland, Maryland

Hike 21
Oldtown to
Cumberland

Hike 20
Paw Paw to
Oldtown

Hike 19
Little Orleans to
Paw Paw

Hike 18
Hancock to
Little Orleans

Hike 17
Fort Frederick
State Park to
Hancock

Hike 16
Williamsport to
Fort Frederick
State Park

Hike 15
Dam 4 to
Williamsport

Hike 14
Shepherdstown
to Dam 4

Hike 13
Harpers Ferry
to Shepherdstown

PENNSYLVANIA

WEST
VIRGINIA

MILES

0   5   10

Canal and
towpath trail

Rapids and
hazardous areas

Boat launch

Restrooms

Picnic area

Drive-in camping area

Telephone

Hiker-biker campsite

Wheelchair accessible

Historic Site

Canal Terminus
Feeder Dam 8
Guard Lock 8

Cumberland
Cumberland Visitor Center

Evitts Creek
Aqueduct

North Branch

Evitts Creek

Locks 74-75
Irons Mountain
Lock 72
Lock 72

Spring Gap   Spring Gap

Pigmans Ferry
Oldtown-Battie Mixon
Lock 71
Oldtown
Locks 69-70

Potomac Forks
Lock 68

Town Creek
Aqueduct
Lock 67

GREEN RIDGE
STATE FOREST

Access to
Green Ridge Trail

Purslane Run
Locks 63-66
Sorrel
Ridge
Tunnel Hill Trail

Locks
62-69

Devils Alley
Little Orleans

Indigo Neck

Lock 60
Paw Paw Tunnel
(3,118 ft long)

Stickpile
Hill
Fifteenmile
Creek
Aqueduct

Sideling Hill Creek Aqueduct
Lock 58

Locks 54-55
Cacapon
Junction
Lock
53

Great Cacapon

Leopards Mill

Berkeley Springs

Little Tonoloway
Tonoloway Creek
Aqueduct

Hancock
Hancock Visitor Center

Locks 51-52

Little Pool

Access to Tuscarora Trail

Licking Creek
Aqueduct

Access to Western
Maryland Rail Trail

Big Pool   Big Pool
FORT FREDERICK STATE PARK

McCoys Ferry

North
Mountain

Locks
47-50

Four Locks
Lock 46
Dam 5 Lock 45

Dam 5

Jordan
Junction

Martinsburg

Cumberland Valley
Midpoint of C&O Canal
Opequon Junction

Lock
43
Lock 42

Potomac
Edison
Dam

Conococheague
Creek
Aqueduct
Williamsport Visitor Center

Lock 41

Williamsport

Hagerstown

Hedgesville

Big Slackwater
Guard Lock 4

Snyders Landing
Barron's C & O Museum

Killiansburg Cave

Shepherdstown
Ranger Station
Pack Horse Ford

Lock 40

Dam 4

Big Woods
Taylors Landing

Horseshoe
Bend

Sharpsburg

Lock 39

Charles Town

Antietam Creek
(walk-in camp)

Dargan Bend

Huckleberry Hill

Dam 3 Lock 37
Locks 35-38
Lock
Duncan

Lock 36

Antietam
Creek
Aqueduct

ANTIETAM
NATIONAL
BATTLEFIELD

Antietam
National
Battlefield

Boonesboro

Harpers Ferry
Lock 35
Lock 34

HARPERS FERRY
NATIONAL HISTORICAL
PARK

WEST
VIRGINIA

Footbridge

Lock 33

Lock 32

VIRGINIA

Appalachian Trail

Appalachian Trail

56

Hike 13
Along the C&O Canal Towpath
Harpers Ferry to Lock 38, Shepherdstown

Starting at the 1893 railroad trestle, the westbound towpath now enters one of its most dramatic sections. On your right, towering cliffs dwarf the canal. Until the early 1950s, wild goats roamed the wooded ridge. Black bears have been making a comeback in the area as well—making their way back just as human settlement is expanding rapidly. The Potomac roars through a set of Class II rapids known as The Needles. Look for kayakers along here. After hiking a mile north of Harpers Ferry, you re-enter woods and soon reach Feeder Dam 3 and the ruins of a lockhouse and a drydock. Soon you come to the beautifully restored Antietam Aqueduct. The section ends at the trailhead near Shepherdstown, WV.

TRIP PLANNER

Start: Harpers Ferry.
End: Shepherdstown.
Miles: 11.8
Points of Interest: Harpers Ferry; Maryland Heights Trail; Feeder Dam 3; Antietam Aqueduct; Shepherdstown.
Parking: Lock 34 (0.9 mi.); Dargan Bend Recreation Area (4.2 mi.); Mountain Lock Recreation Area (6.5 mi.); Antietam Creek Campsite (8.8 mi.); Lock 38 (12.1 mi.).
Water: Huckleberry Hill Antietam Creek Campsites.
Restroom or Privy: Huckleberry Hill; Dargan Bend; Mountain Lock Recreation Area; Antietam Creek Campsite.
Provisions: Harpers Ferry, limited; Shepherdstown.
Camping: Huckleberry Hill and Antietam Creek Campsites.

HIKE DATA

0.0   Harpers Ferry. You can access town by climbing the spiral staircase to the walkway that carries the AT across the Potomac River. From Harpers Ferry, the Appalachian Trail heads south to Georgia. Harpers Ferry National Historical Park features restored buildings, exhibits, a visitor center and bookstore. Restrooms and water are available during park hours.
0.6   Footbridge to Maryland Heights Trail.
0.9   Lock 34.
1.6   Feeder Dam 3 and Lock 35.
2.2   Huckleberry Hill Campsite.
4.2   Dargan Bend Recreation Area. There is a day use picnic area, no camping.

6.3   Lock 37.

8.7   Antietam Aqueduct.

8.8   Antietam Campsite.

11.8   Shepherdstown Trailhead. To reach town follow trail from parking lot 0.3 miles to the bridge over the Potomac. The town is just across the river.

EXPLORING THE TOWPATH CORRIDOR
Harpers Ferry. See Hike 12 on page 52.

Maryland Heights Trail. This trail is accessed from the towpath a quarter mile north of the footbridge across the river at Harpers Ferry. The route starts as a very steep climb up an old woods road but is well worth the effort. The trail visits stone forts, trenches and other Civil War ruins. One leg of trail reaches the cliff above the Harpers Ferry Tunnel. Hikes of up to four to six miles are possible; or take the half-hour hike to the overlook. Sturdy footwear is advisable and extra caution is needed in inclement weather. Maps of this trail are available at the Harpers Ferry Visitor Center on Shenandoah Street in Harpers Ferry.

Antietam Battlefield. The park surrounds the town of Sharpsburg, Maryland. On September 17, 1862, more than 23,000 men died here in the bloodiest battle in U.S. history. Walking tours of the battlefield and the cemetery bring that grim day to life. The village of Sharpsburg contains historic buildings, a civil war artifacts shop, two cafés and an ice cream scoop shop. To reach the battlefield, leave the towpath at Snyders Landing Road and go 1.6 miles to Route 65 in Sharpsburg. Turn left and go one mile north to battlefield.

Shepherdstown. This picturesque village is the oldest town in West Virginia. German Street features a terrific bookstore, a bakery, tea room, coffee shop, beer and wine store, and boutiques. It has an array of casual and upscale eateries, a B&B and dozens of historic structures. On Route 45, a half-mile west of the four-way stop, there is a motel and grocery store. Shepherdstown is also the home of the Contemporary American Theater Festival each July and the American Conservation Film Festival in autumn. On December 3, 1787, inventor James Rumsey successfully demonstrated his steamboat here, an event commemorated with a park and monument high above the river.

Hike 14
Along the C&O Canal
Shepherdstown to Dam 4

West of Shepherdstown, the canal passes beneath beautiful cliffs for about four miles. This area contains several caves, including Killiansburg Cave, where people from the area took refuge during the Battle of Antietam. Further west, farmland returns and a peaceful walk takes you past the village of Mercersville, through the "Big Woods" to the winch house at Dam 4.

TRIP PLANNER
Start: Trailhead parking area east of Shepherdstown.
End: Dam 4.
Miles: 11.9
Points of Interest: Shepherdstown; Barron's C&O Museum; Mercersville (Taylor's Landing); Dam 4.
Parking: Lock 38 (0.0 mi.); Snyder's Landing (4.2 mi.); Dam 4 (11.6 mi.).
Water: Killiansburg Cave, Horseshoe Bend, Big Woods Campsite; Dam 4.
Restroom or Privy: Killiansburg Cave, Horseshoe Bend, Big Woods Campsite; Dam 4.
Provisions: Shepherdstown; Barron's Museum (limited snacks on weekend).

TRIP PLANNER
0.0   The Shepherdstown Trailhead is 0.3 miles downstream of the Route 34 bridge.
0.3   Lock 38 at Shepherdstown.
2.7   Killiansburg Cave Campsite.
4.2   Snyder's Landing.
4.3   Barron's Museum, located across road from canal. Open on weekends throughout the year.
7.4   Horseshoe Bend Campsite.
8.4   Taylor's Landing (Mercersville), no services here.
10.1 Big Woods Campsite.
11.9 Dam 4 and winch house. A mandatory 4.7-mile detour west to McMahon's Mill begins here. On bicycle, it is a lovely ride. On foot, it is a tedious detour for end-to-end hikers.

EXPLORING THE PHT
Shepherdstown. See Hike 14 on page 58.
Dam 4. This area features the only remaining winch house on the canal. Its purpose was to lower a stop gate (similar to the one at Great Falls) if flooding occurred upstream. The dam overlook makes a fine picnic spot and serves as an entry to the Big Slackwater area. For 3.3 miles upstream from the inlet lock, no canal was built. Instead, boats used the calm, slackwater section of the Potomac until they re-entered the canal above McMahon's Mill. You can explore the area on the service road

and a rough stretch of towpath above the dam. It's a peaceful and unique scene; but you cannot proceed upriver on the towpath beyond the dam. Westbound hikers must take a 4.7 mile detour that begins at Dam 4 and rejoins at the McMahon's Mill. To proceed west, cross the canal and turn right, following road uphill. Towpath signs lead the way.

Hike 15
Along the C&O Canal
Dam 4 to Williamsport

This segment begins with a 4.7 mile road walk, but you can explore the area around the dam before starting out. The road walk is scenic and, despite the winding road, relatively safe. At the end of the road walk, a restored 1778 mill sits by the Potomac. For the next 0.8 miles the towpath passes beneath towering limestone cliffs at the upper end of Big Slackwater. Caves, including the well-known Howell Caves, dot the cliffs here. At the inlet lock (Lock 41) the canal resumes and soon enters the half-mile Dellinger Widewater. Past here, cliffs, often a hundred feet high, continue to near milepost 93. For a mile, the towpath is a paved road through the summer home community of Falling Water. Soon the woods return and the towpath passes through a quiet section to the village of Williamsport.

TRIP PLANNER

Start: Dam 4.
End: Williamsport.
Miles: 16.4
Points of Interest: Dam 4; McMahon's Mill; Big Slackwater; Dellinger Widewater; Williamsport.
Parking: Dam 4 (0.0 mi.); Lock 44 (15.9 mi.); Williamsport (16.4 mi.).
Water: Opequon Junction and Cumberland Valley Campsites; Williamsport; (water at campsites normally turned off November through April).
Restroom or Privy: Dam 4; Opequon Junction and Cumberland Valley Campsites; Williamsport.
Provisions: Williamsport.
Camping: Opequon Junction and Cumberland Valley Campsites.

HIKE DATA

0.0   Dam 4 and winch house. A mandatory 4.7-mile detour west to McMahon's Mill begins here. Cross the canal, turn right and follow Dam 4 Road.
3.5   Dellinger Road. Turn left.
3.9   Avis Mill Road. Turn left.
4.7   McMahon's Mill. Cross the canal and turn right on towpath.
7.5   Opequon Junction Campsite.
11.8 Cumberland Valley Campsite.
15.9 Lock 44.
16.4 Williamsport, Md.

EXPLORING THE PHT

Williamsport. In 1790, extra wide streets were built as part of the town's campaign to be selected as the Nation's Capital. President George Washington came here October 14 of that year to discuss the proposal with town founder Otho Williams. The bid failed because the Potomac River was not navigable for large ships this far upstream. During the canal's operating period, Williamsport was the center of canal life. Many canalers wintered here. Cushwa's Warehouse, beside the canal, has been restored as a visitors center containing exhibits and canal artifacts. Among the historic structures in town is Wolfe's On the Square; the store is filled with canal history and is owned by the family of C&O boatman George "Hooper" Wolfe. Motels are located about one mile north on Route 11.

Hike 16
Along the C&O Canal
Williamsport to Fort Frederick State Park

Leaving Williamsport, the trail crosses the Conococheague Aqueduct. In April 1920, the sidewall of this aqueduct collapsed, sending a boat tumbling into the creek. A temporary wooden wall was constructed and remained in place until the canal closed in 1924.

Upstream from town, woods and cornfields give way to a distant roar as you approach Dam 5. For nearly 20 years this was the head of canal navigation, and the nearby community still boasts the dam's name. Further upstream, the towpath enters Little Slackwater. Unlike its "big brother" to the east, this area has been repaired and is one of the highlights of the canal. Next comes Four Locks and the McCoys Ferry area. Then the woods and the deer get thicker. The hike ends just south of Fort Frederick State Park at the entrance to Big Pool.

TRIP PLANNER

Start: Williamsport.

End: Fort Frederick State Park.

Miles: 12.6

Points of Interest: Williamsport, Cushwa Visitor Center and Conococheague Aqueduct; Dam 5 and Little Slackwater; Four Locks; Fort Frederick State Park.

Parking: Cushwa Visitor Center (0.0 mi.); Dam 5 (7.0 mi.); Four Locks (8.7 mi.) McCoy's Ferry CG (10.7 mi.); Fort Frederick State Park (12.6 mi.).

Water: Cushwa Visitor Center; Jordan Junction Campsite; North Mountain Campsite; Fort Frederick State Park; (water at campsites normally turned off November through April).

Restroom or Privy: Cushwa Visitor Center; Jordan Junction Campsite; Dam 5; North Mountain Campsite; McCoys Ferry CG; Fort Frederick State Park.

Provisions: Williamsport; Fort Frederick State Park, a snack bar daily April through September, weekends in October.

Camping: Jordan Junction and North Mountain campsites; McCoys Ferry campground; Fort Frederick State Park.

HIKE DATA

0.0   Williamsport. Within a few blocks the towpath find groceries, cafes and restaurants.

1.5   Jordan Junction Campsite. Tent sites are in a scenic location across from a cornfield.

7.0	Dam 5. The cluster of houses here is the community known as Dam Number 5, Md.
7.0	Little Slackwater. This is a scenic area, where the towpath has been restored.
7.5	Canal resumes.
8.7	Four Locks. The canal cuts across Prather's Neck here to avoid bends of the Potomac.
10.2	North Mountain campsite.
10.7	McCoys Ferry Drive-In Campground.
12.6	Fort Frederick State Park. To visit the park turn right at canal milepost 112.4. The fort is about a half mile up the park road.

EXPLORING THE TOWPATH CORRIDOR
Williamsport. See Hike 15 on page 60.

Four Locks. This series of locks was needed to cut across Prather's Neck, thereby, avoiding a four-mile bend in the Potomac. Today, there is much to explore, starting with the ruins of Charles Mill just east of the locks. Other structures here include a mule barn, Four Locks and a wait house, where the lock tender could get out of the weather. The lockhouse is now used as a ranger station. There are picnic facilities and good access to the river.

Fort Frederick State Park. This fort was built in 1756 to protect English settlers during the French and Indian War. Its stone construction was rare for the period; most forts were built of earth and wood. By the 1920s, the walls were near ruin. In the 1930s the Civilian Conservation Corps restored the outer walls. Today, restoration activity continues inside the fort, and tours are available. The grounds feature paths to explore. Down by the river a boat ramp and campground are available. Rental boats are available for paddling around Big Pool. Just a half mile west of the park, in the village of Big Pool, is the eastern terminus of the 23-mile Western Maryland Rail Trail.

Hike 17
Along the C&O Canal
Fort Frederick State Park to Hancock

This section of the canal is dominated by two large lakes, Big Pool and Little Pool. The first was formed by taking advantage of a natural ridge to create a lake. To create Big Pool, canal builders cut through the ridge and let the river flood the low area behind it. Both areas are excellent locations for birding and watching wildlife.

Beyond Big Pool the canal is lined with cornfields. Watch for deer in the evenings. Just past Big Pool, cross Ernstville Road in the community of Ernstville. A sign directs hikers to the Western Maryland Rail Trail a hundred yards north. That trail parallels the C&O Canal all the way to Hancock, with a direct connection at the east end of Little Pool. Further on, Licking Creek Aqueduct is the backdrop for a campsite by the same name. Just beyond, the 255-mile Tuscarora Trail joins from the north. The two trails share an alignment to Hancock.

TRIP PLANNER

Start: Fort Frederick State Park.

End: Hancock.

Miles: 11.7

Points of Interest: Fort Frederick State Park; Big Pool; Licking Creek Aqueduct; Tuscarora Trail; Little Pool; Western Maryland Rail Trail; Hancock.

Parking: Fort Frederick State Park (0.0 mi.); Hancock (11.7 mi.).

Water: Fort Frederick State Park; Licking Creek and Little Pool Campsites; Hancock.

Restroom or Privy: Fort Frederick State Park; Licking Creek and Little Pool Campsites; Hancock.

Provisions: Fort Frederick State Park snack bar is open daily April through September; weekends in October.

Camping: Fort Frederick State Park; Licking Creek and Little Pool Campsites.

HIKE DATA

0.0   Fort Frederick State Park. To visit the park, turn right onto the park road at canal milepost 112.4.

0.1   Big Pool.

2.1   Ernstville. Access to Western Maryland Rail Trail. No services here.

3.6   Licking Creek Aqueduct.

3.8   Licking Creek Campsite.

3.8   Tuscarora Trail joins from the north. It follows the towpath west to the Route 522 bridge in Hancock.

7.4   Little Pool. This is an old channel of the river. Access the Western Maryland Rail Trail here via a set of steps just across a footbridge.

10.6 Tonoloway Creek Aqueduct.

11.7 Hancock. Shops, restaurants and motels are within a few blocks of the canal. The State of Maryland is barely a mile wide here. Hikers can access the southbound Tuscarora Trail via the Route 522 bridge.

EXPLORING THE TOWPATH CORRIDOR

Fort Frederick State Park. See Hike 16 on page 62.

Hancock. The village serves as the base for a variety of outdoor activities. The C&O Canal, Tuscarora, and Western Maryland trails merge in town, making this an ideal spot to start or end a trip. Hancock features restaurants and a bakery only steps from the towpath. The river can be accessed here as well. Just above the trailhead is a restaurant with a bar serving up microbrews.

Tuscarora Trail. This trail links to the Appalachian Trail (AT) in Virginia and Pennsylvania to form a 450-mile loop. It was built in the late 1960s as a potential replacement route for the existing AT when trail planners were concerned that development and military installations might disrupt the route. Today the Tuscarora offers a rugged 255-mile route to explore.

Western Maryland Rail Trail. This 23-mile trail offers a unique chance for a different view of the canal area. Historic markers along the route tell the stories of villages and stations lost to time. Despite the proximity to the canal, the rail trail offers an entirely different experience. West of Hancock, the trail climbs rapidly through massive rock cuts.

Hike 18
Along the C&O Canal
Hancock to Little Orleans

At the west end of Hancock, the trail passes ruins of the Round Top Cement Mill. West of here the trail enters the mountains, with Capacon and Round Top coming into view. Above the canal, telegraph poles march west along the Western Maryland Grade. On the West Virginia side of the Potomac, CSX trains pass regularly. At night it is interesting to watch their giant headlights from camp. At Indigo Neck, the towpath traces a long arc while the abandoned Western Maryland Railroad passes through the 4,350-foot Indigo Tunnel. This wild and beautiful section ends at the Fifteenmile Creek Campground in Little Orleans. Be sure to visit Bill's Place just through the railroad underpass. It is a favorite among trail travelers.

TRIP PLANNER
Start: Hancock.
End: Little Orleans.
Miles: 16.7
Points of Interest: Hancock; Round Top Cement Mill; Sideling Hill Aqueduct; Indigo Tunnel; Little Orleans.
Parking: Hancock (0.0 mi.); Fifteenmile Creek Campground (16.7 mi.).
Water: Hancock; White Rock Campsite; Leopards Mill, Cacapon Junction, and Indigo Neck Campsites; Fifteenmile Creek Campground.
Restroom or Privy: White Rock, Leopards Mill, Cacapon Junction and Indigo Neck Campsites; Fifteenmile Creek Campground.
Provisions: Hancock; Little Orleans (restaurant and limited supplies).
Camping: White Rock, Leopards Mill, Cacapon Junction, and Indigo Neck Campsites; Fifteenmile Creek Campground.

HIKE DATA
0.0 Hancock. Access the southbound Tuscarora Trail via the Route 522 bridge.
2.4 White Rocks Campsite.
3.3 Ruins of Round Top Cement Mill. Much of the cement used in canal structures was produced here.
5.8 Leopards Mill Campsite.
9.5 Cacapon Junction Campsite. This is a beautiful location across from the Cacapon River in West Virginia. There is a fine arched railroad bridge across from camp.
12.1 Pearre.
12.5 Sideling Hill Creek Aqueduct. Connection with Western Maryland Rail Trail.
15.0 Indigo Neck Campsite.
16.7 Little Orleans, Maryland and Fifteenmile Creek Campground. The settlement is named for the B&O's Orleans Crossroads across the Potomac. To visit Bill's Place, turn right at Fifteenmile Creek Camp ground and pass under the Western Maryland.

Bill's Place. Bill's place is the center of life in this quiet corner. Have a burger and a beer, then sit on the porch and watch time go by. If you want to memorialize your visit, bring a buck for the ceiling.

Hike 19
Along the C&O Canal
Little Orleans to Paw Paw

This is the wildest, most remote section of the C&O Canal Towpath. At Little Orleans the towpath crosses Fifteenmile Creek Aqueduct and clings to the river as it heads upstream. For the most part, the berm is folded rock. In some sections the abandoned Western Maryland grade looms over the canal. At three different places, massive trestles carry the tracks across the river. Look for turtles in the watered portions of the canal, basking on snags on sunny days.

Further west, the mountains close in. Near Tunnel Hollow, the route enters a deep cut leading to the Paw Paw Tunnel. Emerging from the tunnel the sections ends at Route 51, just across the river from Paw Paw, West Virginia.

TRIP PLANNER

Start: Little Orleans.
End: Paw Paw.
Miles: 15.4
Points of Interest: Little Orleans; Green Ridge Hiking Trail; Tunnel Hollow; Tunnel Hill Trail; Paw Paw Tunnel.
Parking: Fifteenmile Creek Campground (0.0 mi.); Paw Paw (15.4 mi.).
Water: Fifteenmile Creek Campground; Devils Alley, Stickpile Hill, Sorrel Ridge, and Paw Paw Tunnel Campsites.
Restroom or Privy: Fifteenmile Creek Campground; Devils Alley, Stickpile Hill, Sorrel Ridge, and Paw Paw Tunnel Campsites.
Provisions: Little Orleans (restaurant plus limited supplies); Paw Paw (restaurants and limited supplies).
Camping: Fifteenmile Creek Campground; Devils Alley, Stickpile Hill, Sorrel Ridge, and Paw Paw Tunnel Campsites.

HIKE DATA

0.0 Little Orleans. and Fifeenmile Creek Campground. The settlement is named for the B&O's Orleans Crossroads across the Potomac.
0.1 Fifteen Mile Creek Aqueduct.

2.5	Western Maryland trestle. This is the first of nine trestles that cross the Potomac between here and Cumberland.
3.1	Lock 58 and Green Ridge Hiking Trail. The trail adjacent to Green Ridge State Forest.
3.7	Devils Alley Campsite. The origin of the name is not known, but to campers it is an apt description of the cold winds that blow here.
6.4	Western Maryland Railroad trestle.
8.6	Stickpile Hill Campsite. The campsite takes its name from the nearby Western Maryland Stickpile Tunnel. Legend has it that a hobo was killed on the tracks and buried under a pile of sticks in a lonely grave.
10.4	Western Maryland Railroad trestle.
13.3	Sorrel Ridge Campsite. Nestled in a wild place next to the ruins of an old lockhouse.
13.7	Lock 63 1/3. Fractional numbers are used at this and the next lock because Lock 65 was never built.
13.8	Lock 64 2/3.
14.0	Tunnel Hill Trail. A 1.5 mile route that passes over the ridge with good views of Paw Paw Bends in winter. It rejoins the canal at the tunnel's west portal.
14.4	Paw Paw Tunnel. This is a special place anytime, but especially on a cold day when massive ice hangs from the rock cut called Tunnel Hollow.
15.1	Paw Paw Tunnel Campsite.
15.4	Route 51. The town of Paw Paw has a convenience store and a restaurant about 0.8 miles from the canal. To reach town, turn left and cross the river.

EXPLORING THE PHT
Little Orleans. See Hike 19 on page 67.
Green Ridge State Forest. There are more than 45,000 acres to explore. The Green Ridge Trail winds for nearly 20 miles between Lock 58 and Lock 67, where it rejoins the C&O Canal. The trail winds in and out of deep hollows through mixed pine, oak and hickory forest. The hollows feature canyons of slate and shale where old logging grades are utilized for the route. Camping shelters are available. This region is home to all manner of wildlife including black bear. Seven miles north of Lock 58, the Pine Lick Trail leaves the main loop and extends north six miles to the Pennsylvania line. Here it links to the Mid State Trail which extends 261 miles to Blackwell, Pennsylvania. Work is underway to extend this trail to New York.

Paw Paw Tunnel. It took nearly 14 years to dig the tunnel, which was completed in 1850, opening the canal to Cumberland. Tunnel Hollow is a massive cut through shale that is held in place with rods embedded in the rock. Springs seep everywhere creating spectacular ice formations in the winter. Just before the west end of the tunnel, a trail climbs away from the towpath. This was actually built during the 1830s as a tunnel construction road, making it one of the oldest trails in the country. The tunnel is lined with bricks six deep. At 3,118 feet, it was the second longest canal tunnel ever built in the U.S. Only the Big Tunnel on the Sandy & Beaver Canal in Ohio is longer.

Hike 20
Along the C&O Canal
Paw Paw to Oldtown

This quiet section is bounded by cliffs along the Western Maryland grade and by the lockhouses in the Oldtown area. Much of the section is watered, either through restoration or by busy beavers. This is a good area to spot deer and other wildlife. From Town Creek aqueduct to Lock 71, anglers wade the waters on weekends. At Lock 67, the Green Ridge Hiking Trail returns to the towpath. It heads back east some 17.8 miles to Lock 58, providing a backpacking route. This hike ends by Lock 70 in Oldtown, just uphill from the last private toll bridge across the Potomac.

TRIP PLANNER
Start: Paw Paw.
End: Oldtown.
Miles: 10.4
Points of Interest: Paw Paw; Town Creek Aqueduct; Oldtown.
Parking: Paw Paw (0.0); Oldtown (10.4 mi.).
Water: Paw Paw; Purslane Run, Town Creek and Potomac Forks Campsites.
Restroom or Privy: Paw Paw; Purslane Run, Town Creek and Potomac Forks Campsites.
Provisions: Paw Paw (0.75 miles across river in West Virginia); Oldtown (0.5 miles into town).
Camping: Purslane Run, Town Creek and Potomac Forks Campsites.

HIKE DATA
0.0   Paw Paw, W.Va. To reach town, turn left and cross the river.
0.6   Purslane Run Campsite.
5.5   Lock 67. The Green Ridge Hiking Trail rejoins the towpath here.
5.9   Town Creek Campsite.
6.1   Town Creek Aqueduct.
8.6   Potomac Forks Campsite. This is the only campsite on the canal on the berm side of the towpath.
10.4 Oldtown and Lock 70. Town is about 0.5 miles to the right at canal milepost 166.7. There is one small general store. Turn left here for private toll bridge across the Potomac.

EXPLORING THE PHT
Oldtown. The lockhouses at three of the four Oldtown locks (68, 70 and 71) have been restored. There is a small museum at Lockhouse 70. Just down the hill is a private, low-water toll bridge, built in 1937, that crosses the Potomac to Green Spring, West Virginia. The toll is 50 cents. Fishing is a popular activity here; this section of the canal is stocked by the Maryland Department of Natural Resources. The town's name has survived from the 1700s when it was known as Shawnee Oldtown for the departed Indian tribe.

Hike 21
Along the C&O Canal
Oldtown to Cumberland
The final segment of the PHT along the C&O Canal starts with an interesting passage through the Alum Hill Deep Cut. Sheer walls of crumbling shale rise above the towpath. Beyond the cut, the towpath

enters a meadow at the former site of Pigman's Ferry. From here to Spring Gap the canal passes through quiet woods. West of the gap the trail passes the ruins of a water supply pumping system and Blue Spring, one of the largest springs in the Eastern U.S. Just a few yards further is Lock 72 in an area known as The Narrows, with a fine two story lockhouse and full porch. At the head of The Narrows, the final three locks complete the 605-foot climb from Georgetown. The remaining distance to Cumberland is pleasant, with increasing signs of civilization at each mile. The final aqueduct is crossed 4.5 miles from Cumberland, and sets up a grand finish. The church spires and buildings, with the Allegheny Mountains as a backdrop, guide you to the restored Western Maryland depot.

Photo by Paul g. Wiegman

TRIP PLANNER

Start: Oldtown.

End: Cumberland.

Miles: 17.8

Points of Interest: Oldtown; Alum Hill Deep Cut; Lock 75; Evitts Creek Aqueduct; Western Maryland Depot and canal terminus.

Parking: Oldtown (0.0 mi.); Spring Gap (6.7 mi.); Lock 74 (8.8 mi.); Candoc Recreation Area (15.1 mi.); Western Maryland Depot (17.8 mi.).

Water: Pigman's Ferry; Irons Mt. and Evitts Creek Campsites; Cumberland.

Restroom or Privy: Pigman's Ferry; Irons Mt. and Evitts Creek Campsites; Cumberland.

Provisions: Oldtown (store 0.5 miles north in town); Cumberland.
Camping: Pigman's Ferry; Irons Mt. and Evitts Creek Campsites.

HIKE DATA

0.0   Oldtown and Lock 70. There is one small general store.
0.8   Alum Hill Deep Cut. Walls of pencil-thin shards of shale rise above the towpath in this area.
2.5   Pigman's Ferry Campsite. This is the only canal campsite situated in an open meadow. Expect wildlife activity at night and a damp tent in the morning.
6.7   Spring Gap.
8.6   Irons Mountain Campsite.
8.8   Lock 74.
13.3 Evitts Creek Campsite.
14.0 Evitts Creek Aqueduct.
15.1 Candoc Recreation Area. Candoc is an acronym for C&O Canal.
17.8 Cumberland C&O Canal Place Visitor Center. To continue on the Great Allegheny Passage, another segment of the PHT, follow the tracks of the Western Maryland Scenic Railroad north from the station. Cumberland is served by both Greyhound and Amtrak.

EXPLORING THE TOWPATH CORRIDOR
Oldtown. See Hike 20 on page 69.
Cumberland. October 10, 1850 was the celebration of the canal's completion. William Price, a Cumberland lawyer, gave a speech which might have surprised the VIPs in the audience. "Many of us were young when this great work was commenced, and we have lived to see its completion only because Providence has prolonged our lives until our heads are gray. Thousands have been ruined by their connection with this work and but few in this region have any cause to bless it." Today the city is an excellent hub in the PHT network, with daily train and bus service. The scenic train between Cumberland and Frostburg follows 16 miles of the Great Allegheny Passage.

RESOURCES
Amtrak
(800) 872-7245
www.amtrak.com

Allegheny Trail Alliance
888-ATA-BIKE (282-2453)
www.atatrail.org

Antietam National Battlefield
(301) 423-5124
www.nps.gov/anti

Appalachian Trail Conservancy
(304) 535-6331
www.appalachiantrail.org

Barron's C&O Museum
(301) 432-8726

Bill's Place
(301) 478-2828

C&O Canal Visitor Center (NPS)
(301) 722-8226
www.nps.gov/choh

Williamsport Visitor Center (NPS)
(301) 582-0813

Fort Frederick State Park
(301) 842-2155

Green Ridge State Forest
(301) 478-3124
www.state.dnr.md.us

Greyhound
(800) 231-2222
Hancock Visitor Center (NPS)
(301) 678-5463

MARC Trains
(800) 325-7245
www.mtamaryland.com/

Shepherdstown Visitor Center
(304) 876-2786

Western Maryland Scenic Railroad
(800) TRAIN 50
www.wmsr.com

GREAT ALLEGHENY PASSAGE:
CUMBERLAND TO OHIOPYLE

C oal, minerals and timber extracted from these mountains made
their way into Cumberland on narrow-gauge railroads. The region's
abundant natural resources and its location on the river made
Cumberland one of America's early industrial centers. The wares made
there were shipped east along the railroad and canal. Then, as now, nearly
all traffic west goes along the steep hillside above Braddock Run.

The one that does not, the corridor of the Western Maryland Railroad,
provides a spectacular passage above Jennings Run. It is today the route
of the Western Maryland Scenic Railroad and the Great Allegheny Passage,
which follows the rail line to Frostburg. The trail then heads northwest up
and through Big Savage Mountain, along tributaries of the Youghiogheny
River to the River's main stem at Confluence.

The Great Allegheny Passage (GAP) trail system between Cumberland
and Pittsburgh is a great conservation story. The people leading the effort
are known collectively as the Allegheny Trail Alliance. In 2003, the GAP
was designated a segment of the Potomac Heritage National Scenic Trail
and is destined to become one of the best-loved multi-use trails in
America. You'll see white mile posts along the **completed** sections of the

Photo by Paul g. Wiegman

Great Allegheny Passage. They note the distance from Cumberland—Cumberland will be Milepost 0 and Pittsburgh's Point will be Milepost 150. The highland views from Big Savage Mountain, the riverside trail in the lower elevations, and the varied countryside draw thousands of visitors. For many people, the top draw is the restored Big Savage Tunnel. (The tunnel lights are on from 6 am to 9 pm. The tunnel is closed from late November to early April to protect it from the elements.) For hikers seeking solitude, the best bet for hiking Frostburg to Ohiopyle will be early mornings and late afternoons or, better still, the cooler months. One of the most delightful ways of all to enjoy the Great Allegheny Passage on foot might be to strap on cross-country skis.

Hike 22
Along the Western Maryland Scenic Railroad
Cumberland to Frostburg

How's this sound for a day in the mountains of Western Maryland? You can walk this segment in the morning, have lunch in Frostburg, then take the scenic railroad back to Cumberland. This entire segment follows the tracks of the Western Maryland Scenic Railroad. In most places you can walk next to the tracks on ballast or dirt. It climbs steadily from Cumberland to a pinch in the mountains called The Narrows, then takes you on a scenic walk through a long horseshoe curve called Helmstetters Curve. Next comes the 963-foot Brush Tunnel. From here just follow the tracks to the Frostburg Depot.

Caution: As this book is going to press in Summer 2006, the Cumberland to Woodcock Hollow section of the Great Allegheny Passage is under construction and closed to trail users. It is anticipated that it will be completed in early 2007.

TRIP PLANNER
Start: Canal Place, Cumberland.
End: Frostburg Depot.
Miles: 16.0
Points of Interest: Cumberland (0.0 mi.); The Narrows (1.0 mi.); Helmstetters Curve (3.0 mi.); Brush Tunnel (6.0 mi.); Frostburg (16.0 mi.).
Parking: Cumberland (0.0 mi.); Frostburg (16.0 mi.).
Water: Cumberland (0.0 mi.); Frostburg (16.0 mi.).
Restroom or Privy: Cumberland (0.0 mi.); Frostburg (16.0 mi.).
Provisions: Cumberland (0.0 mi.); Frostburg (16.0 mi.).
Camping: None.

HIKE DATA

0.0   Cumberland at C&O Canal Place terminus and visitor center. Follow the tracks of the Western Maryland Scenic Railroad north from the station.

1.0   The Narrows. The track clings to a hill here above Alternate Route 40.

3.0   Helmstetters Curve.

6.0   Brush Tunnel. This 963-foot tunnel was built in 1911. The wide gravel path you follow in the tunnel was meant to accommodate a second track, which was never built.

9.0   Woodcock Hollow. As of 2006, the Great Allegheny Passage has been constructed from Woodcock Hollow to McKeesport, Pa. The grade becomes steeper from Woodcock Hollow to the Eastern Continental Divide.

16.0   Frostburg Depot. This depot was part of the old Cumberland & Potomac Railroad. From the depot you are only a short block up the hill to the main street and shops, restaurants and motels. To continue north, follow the switchback path to the Great Allegheny Passage trailhead.

EXPLORE THE PHT CORRIDOR
Cumberland. See Hike 21 on page 70.

Frostburg. This picturesque town is home to Frostburg University. Early development centered around the coming of the National Road in 1811. On the road between Frostburg and Cumberland, reminders of the old National Road include mileposts and the restored LaValle Toll House. By 1863 the last stage coach traveled the road, giving way to the railroad. The first coal mined in Western Maryland came from the Frostburg vicinity in 1846. The historic downtown has been named a National Historic District. You can get to Frostburg by public transportation on Greyhound.

Western Maryland Railroad. Nineteenth century industrialist Jay Gould's Western Maryland line was a latecomer to the railroad scene, not arriving until the early 1900s—the B&O had reached it decades earlier. Instead of following the longer valley routes, the Western Maryland chose direct routes, building tunnels and trestles where necessary. This meant higher maintenance costs and probably contributed to the demise of the line. Today the Western Maryland Scenic Railroad takes countryside visitors from Cumberland to Frostburg. For a multi-modal day of recreation, hike one way and enjoy the train ride back.

Hike 23
Along the Great Allegheny Passage
Frostburg, Md. to Meyersdale, Pa.

From the depot, the Great Allegheny Passage joins the abandoned Western Maryland Connellsville Subdivision, which it will follow to Connellsville. On this section, the highlights include passage over the Eastern Continental Divide at an elevation of 2,375, through the 945-foot Borden Tunnel and over the Mason-Dixon Line into Pennsylvania.

The highlight is the trip through the massive Big Savage Tunnel. Built in 1911, the Big Savage cuts dead straight for nearly 3,300 feet through the mountain. The trail continues north, eventually running next to the active CSX tracks just beyond the Sandpatch Tunnel. Then there is the dramatic 910-foot Keystone Viaduct. The walk ends at the restored Western Maryland Railroad depot in the village of Meyersdale, Pa.

TRIP PLANNER

Start: Frostburg, Md.
End: Meyersdale, Pa.
Miles: 13.0
Points of Interest: Frostburg; Borden Tunnel; Big Savage Tunnel; Keystone Viaduct; Meyersdale, Pa.
Parking: Frostburg (0.0); Meyersdale, Pa. (13.0 mi.); Deal (8.0 mi.).
Water: Frostburg, Md.; Meyersdale, Pa.
Restroom or Privy: Frostburg, Md.; Deal, Pa., Meyersdale, Pa.
Provisions: Frostburg, Md.; Meyersdale, Pa.
Camping: None.

HIKE DATA:

0.0 If you've hiked in from Cumberland to the Frostburg Depot, follow the access trail to the Great Allegheny Passage (GAP) trailhead, about 150 yards downhill. If you're starting in Frostburg, you can park at the GAP trailhead or near the depot.

0.1 Trailhead parking.

0.4 Reach bridge over Route 36.

3.0 Borden Tunnel.

6.8 Big Savage Tunnel.

8.0 Eastern Continental Divide, Deal, Pa.; elevation, 2,375 feet. From here it is downhill to Pittsburgh.

12.0 Keystone Viaduct. This magnificent, curving 910-foot structure crosses Flaugherty Creek.

13.0 Meyersdale, Pa. Turn left at the depot and you are only blocks from shops and restaurants.

EXPLORING THE PHT

Big Savage Tunnel. The tunnel and the trail over the top can be combined for a spectacular 2.5-mile hike. The views from the ridge are well worth the climb. The tunnel takes its name from surveyor Thomas Savage who, along with the rest of the Mayo Expedition, was stranded here in the winter of 1736. According to the legend, he offered himself up as food to save the rest of the party from starving. A rescue team showed up, saving Savage's life. His companions were so grateful that they named the Savage River for him. Fortunately for the traveler of today, food is easier to get now!

Keystone Viaduct. It is not very often that you can sit on one railroad trestle directly above busy, active tracks. This place is a rail fan's dream. The trestle itself is special too; it traces a long curve across the CSX line.

Photo by Bruce Grasser

Meyersdale. Check out the restored depot and stroll down the hill two blocks to Main Street to wander among the historic buildings. This town is unusual in that it was served by competing railroads, a rarity in a small village. The depot has been restored to its 1912 glory.

Hike 24
Along the Great Allegheny Passage
Meyersdale to Rockwood

The PHT leaves Meyersdale and almost immediately reaches the Salisbury Viaduct: 1,908 feet long and 101 feet high. The goal for railroad builders was to cross a broad valley. It was a tough construction job that cost seven men their lives. This is another spot where you can stand above the active CSX line. The Casselman River parallels the trail. It is too shallow for boats, but popular with anglers.

The trail route is almost entirely wooded, but there are interludes through villages, too. Plan your hike to visit each of them. There are cafés, B&Bs, outfitters and bike shops providing services and hospitality to hikers and cyclists.

TRIP PLANNER

Start: Meyersdale.

End: Rockwood.

Miles: 12.0

Points of Interest: Meyersdale; Salisbury Viaduct; Garrett; Rockwood.

Parking: Meyersdale (0.0 mi.); Salisbury Viaduct (1.0 mi.); Garrett (5.0 mi.); Rockwood (12.0 mi.).

Water: Rockwood.

Restroom or Privy: Meyersdale, Garrett, Rockwood.

Provisions: Meyersdale; Garrett; Rockwood.

Camping: None.

HIKE DATA

0.0 Meyersdale. Turn left at the depot and you are only blocks from shops and restaurants. There are B&Bs here as well.

1.0 Salisbury Viaduct. In 2000, the old decking, which had merely been wooden planks laid over the track, was replaced with a concrete walkway.

5.0 Garrett. There is one convenience store. It's easier to walk the 0.3 miles to the store than to describe it: Turn right on Berlin Street to cross the river, then turn right on first side street. Go left under the railroad, right on Route 653 to store. There is also a store on the corner of Route 653 and Route 219.

12.0 Rockwood. Turn right at Bridge Street, Route 653, and follow it across the river and the CSX line to Main Street. There are restaurants, small stores and B&Bs near the trail.

Rockwood. The name Rockwood was chosen by the railroad for the station here. According to the story, after looking at the surrounding terrain and seeing nothing but trees and stone, the name was about as good as they could come up with. Rockwood is a true trail town. It's easy to navigate your way from trail to food and drink and supplies, then get back on the trail. Or you might want to linger awhile. If so, there B&Bs within a few blocks of the trail—one actually is located trailside! Others located a little farther from the trail offer to pick you up at the trailhead.

Hike 25
Along the Great Allegheny Passage
Rockwood to Confluence

The Somerset County section of the Great Allegheny Passage continues to hug the Casselman River. After six miles, the village of Markleton can be reached by a bridge across the Cassleman. Once a hub of activity, Markleton is now a small cluster of houses and a post office; ask for water here. Back across the bridge, next comes the closed Pinkerton Tunnel in a very remote section. The segment ends at the town of Confluence after two grand crossings of the Cassleman River.

TRIP PLANNER

Start: Rockwood.
End: Confluence.
Miles: 18.0
Points of Interest: Rockwood; Markleton; Pinkerton Tunnel; Confluence.
Parking: Rockwood (0.0 mi.); Markleton (6.0 mi.); Fort Hill (12.0 mi.);
    Confluence (18.0 mi.).
Water: Rockwood; Markleton; Confluence.
Restroom or Privy: Rockwood; Markleton; Harnedsville; Confluence.
Provisions: Rockwood; Confluence.
Camping: Confluence.

HIKE DATA

0.0   Rockwood. Turn right at Bridge Street, Route 653, and follow it across the river and the CSX line to Main Street. Restaurants, small stores and B&Bs within a mile of the trail.

6.0   Markleton.

8.0   Pinkerton Tunnel. This tunnel (now closed for repairs) was built for two tracks, but the second track was never built.

12.0 Fort Hill. There are no services here.

16   Harnedsville. There are no supplies here, but there is a B&B less than a mile from the trailhead.

18.0   Confluence. The town has restaurants, B&Bs, food and a pharmacy. Trail services include a campground, bike shop and paddling school. To access them turn right on the pedestrian bridge to cross the Youghiogheny River. All attractions are within a few blocks.

EXPLORING THE AHT CORRIDOR

Markleton. Once there was a pulp mill here that was said to be the largest of its kind in the world. This was one of many "company towns" in the area, in which a company (usually related to logging or mining) laid out a town right at the work site. Houses were leased by the workers, most of whom left when the operation closed down. Markleton included 15 houses, a store, a church, and a stop on the B&O Railroad.

Pinkerton Tunnel. This is a fascinating place to linger. The trail crosses a long trestle and immediately enters Pinkerton Tunnel. Then comes a second, longer trestle. The 849- foot tunnel is closed for repairs so the trail makes a detour of 1.5 miles around the Pinkerton Horn on a temporary track called a "shoofly." It was laid in 1879 by the B&O after the tunnel they built here collapsed in a fire. The track was used until 1885, when the B&O rebuilt their tunnel with brick. There were two tunnels here, serving the Western Maryland and B&O. Track workers

Photo by Paul g. Wiegman

on one tunnel would occasionally be startled to hear a train passing through the other tunnel, only a few feet away. There would always be a momentary alarm when they thought the "ghost train" was coming their way.

Confluence. This town was originally called Turkeyfoot because the three waters which joined here formed that shape. The name was changed to Confluence in the 1870s with the coming of the railroad. Today it is a pleasant place to explore, featuring lodging and restaurants, an outfitter, a paddling school and many interesting structures including two trestles. The campground, bike shop, padding school and one restaurant are along the trail. Head into town by crossing the old Route 281 pedestrian bridge and following River Road to Yough Street which then takes you across a pedestrian bridge and into the town center. There are more restaurants, a hardware store, banks with ATMs and more. All attractions are within a few blocks.

Hike 26
Along the Great Allegheny Passage
Confluence to Ohiopyle

North of Confluence, the Great Allegheny Passage once again becomes a rustic and remote scene of quietly flowing water and dark hemlocks. This is the Youghiogheny River Trail South section of the Great Allegheny Passage.

TRIP PLANNER
Start: Confluence.
End: Ohiopyle.
Miles: 10.5
Points of Interest: Confluence; Ohiopyle.
Parking: Confluence (0.0 mi.); Ramcat (1.8 mi.); Ohiopyle (10.5 mi.).
Water: Confluence; Ohiopyle.
Restroom or Privy: Confluence; Ramcat; Ohiopyle.
Provisions: Confluence; Ramcat snack bar; Ohiopyle.
Camping: Confluence, Ohiopyle.

HIKE DATA
0.0   Confluence.
1.8   Ramcat. Ramcat provides a boat launch and restrooms. There is a small snack bar here.
10.5 Ohiopyle. There is a restroom in the visitor center located in the depot. Other restrooms are near the falls. A general store, B&Bs, hotel and outfitters are all within a few blocks.

EXPLORE THE TRAIL CORRIDOR
Confluence. See Hike 25 on page 80.

Ohiopyle. This little place is a major hub for recreation. It is most famous for whitewater rafting, but there is also a network of short trails. It's a memorable spot for fishing, too. Cross country skiing and snowshoeing offer the best way to solitude in the woods in winter. Just a few miles north on Route 381 is Fallingwater, the famous home built by Frank Lloyd Wright.

RESOURCES
Great Allegheny Passage Somerset Section
(814) 445-1573

Great Allegheny Passage
Allegheny Trail Alliance
(888) ATA-BIKE (282-2453)
www.atatrail.org

Amtrak
(800) 872-7245

C&O Canal Visitor Center (NPS)
(301) 722-8226
www.nps.gov/choh

Allegheny County Tourism Dept.
http://www.mdmountainside.com
(800) 425-2067

Greyhound
(800) 231-2222

Ohiopyle State Park
(724) 329-8591
www.dcnr.state.pa.us/stateparks

Riversport School of Paddling
(800) 216-6991
www.shol.com/kayak/

Western Maryland Scenic Railroad
(800) TRAIN 50
www.wmsr.com

LAUREL HIGHLANDS HIKING TRAIL: OHIOPYLE STATE PARK TO SEWARD, PA.

The Keystone State is laced with long-distance hiking trails that travel deep woods, stream valleys and high mountain ridges. The Laurel Highlands Hiking Trail (LHHT) is thought by many people to be the finest. It is one of few remote backpacking footpaths in the Potomac Heritage National Scenic Trail network. It follows Laurel Ridge through state game lands, forest and other parkland.

Once you've climbed the ridge out of Ohiopyle, the terrain is moderate enough for cross country skiing and snowshoeing. For the hardiest of hikers, there are winter backpacking/skiing trips along the LHHT. Most hikers experience the trail a few hours at a time. With several road crossings, there are plenty of opportunities to hike a few miles out and back, or stash a second car at the next crossing. The Hiking Guide to the Laurel Highlands Trail, published by the Sierra Club, provides natural history and interpretation of the entire 70-mile path. The book is recommended for planning an extended hike on the LHHT.

Photo by Tom Johnson

There are eight camps along the 70-mile trail extending from Ohiopyle to the thousand-foot Conemaugh Gorge near Seward. Each camp has shelters, tent pads, water and privies. Advance registration is required. Along the way, there are hemlock groves, mountain streams, hardwood forests and the sounds of wildlife.

OHIOPYLE FALLS AREA

THIS AREA WAS ORIGINALLY A HUNTING GROUND FOR THE DELAWARE, SHAWNEE AND IROQUOIS INDIANS, WHO NAMED IT "OHIOPEHELLE", MEANING WATER WHITENED BY FROTH. THE YOUGHIOGHENY RIVER WAS NAMED "YOHOGHANY" BY THE INDIANS, MEANING A STREAM FLOWING IN A ROUNDABOUT COURSE.

IN 1754, ON HIS WAY TO WHAT IS NOW PITTSBURGH, GEORGE WASHINGTON CAME THROUGH HERE LOOKING FOR A WATER ROUTE FOR HIS TROOPS AND SUPPLIES, BUT ABANDONED THE IDEA UPON REACHING THE FALLS. AT THIS POINT, THE ELEVATION OF THE RIVERBED DROPS OVER 90 FEET IN ONE MILE.

THE PENINSULA OF LAND ACROSS THE RIVER FROM THE FALLS IS FERNCLIFF WHICH IS A UNIQUE ECOLOGICAL NICHE IN THIS REGION. FERNCLIFF VISITORS MAY USE UP TO FOUR MILES OF NATURE TRAILS TO EXPLORE THE PENINSULA.

SETTLERS MOVED INTO THE AREA ABOUT 1800, AND SINCE THEN THE SETTLEMENT HAS BEEN RENAMED "PILE CITY" IN 1856, WHEN THE FIRST POST OFFICE OPENED, "FALLS CITY" IN 1871 AND "OHIOPYLE" IN 1887. OHIOPYLE WAS INCORPORATED AS A BOROUGH IN 1891. INDUSTRIES HERE HAVE INCLUDED SALTWORKS, COAL MINING, A SAW MILL, A PULP MILL, A SPOKE FACTORY, A "SHOOK" (BARREL COMPONENTS) FACTORY, A GRIST MILL, A TANNERY, AND A WATER WHEEL POWERED ELECTRIC GENERATING PLANT.

Photo by Paul g. Weigman

Hiker's Guide to the
Potomac Heritage Trail
Hikes 27 - 31
Ohiopyle State Park
to
Seward, PA

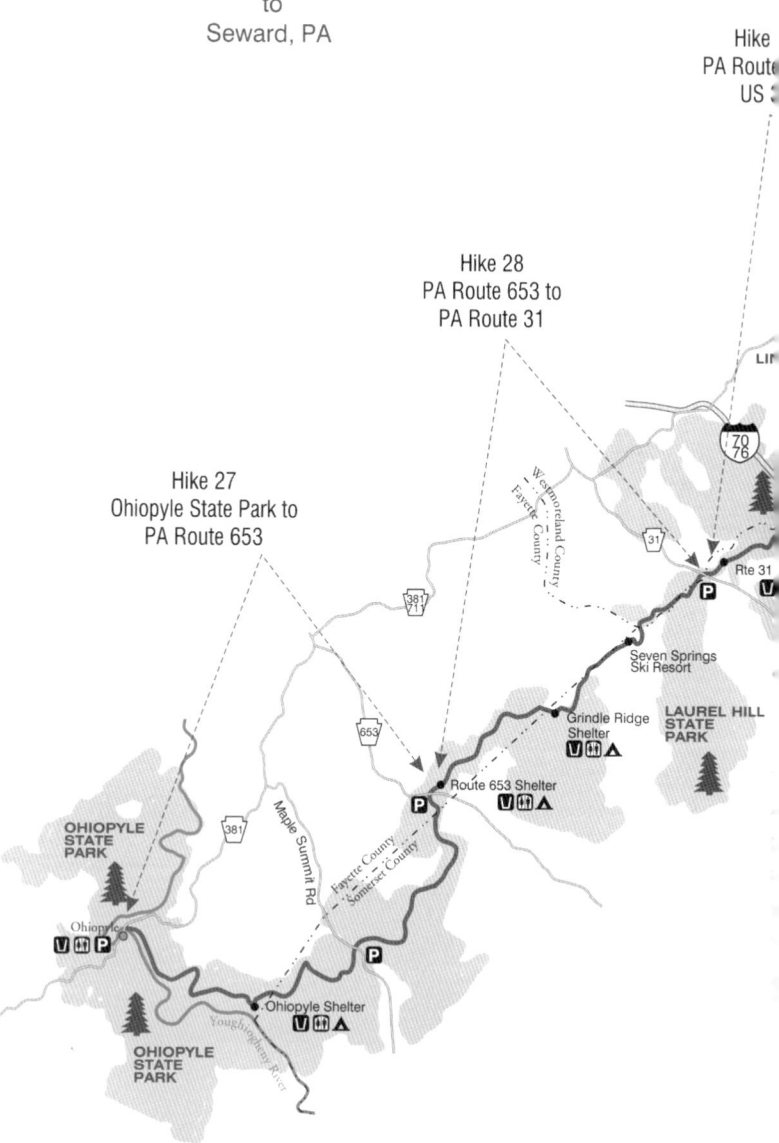

Hike 28
PA Route 653 to
PA Route 31

Hike 27
Ohiopyle State Park to
PA Route 653

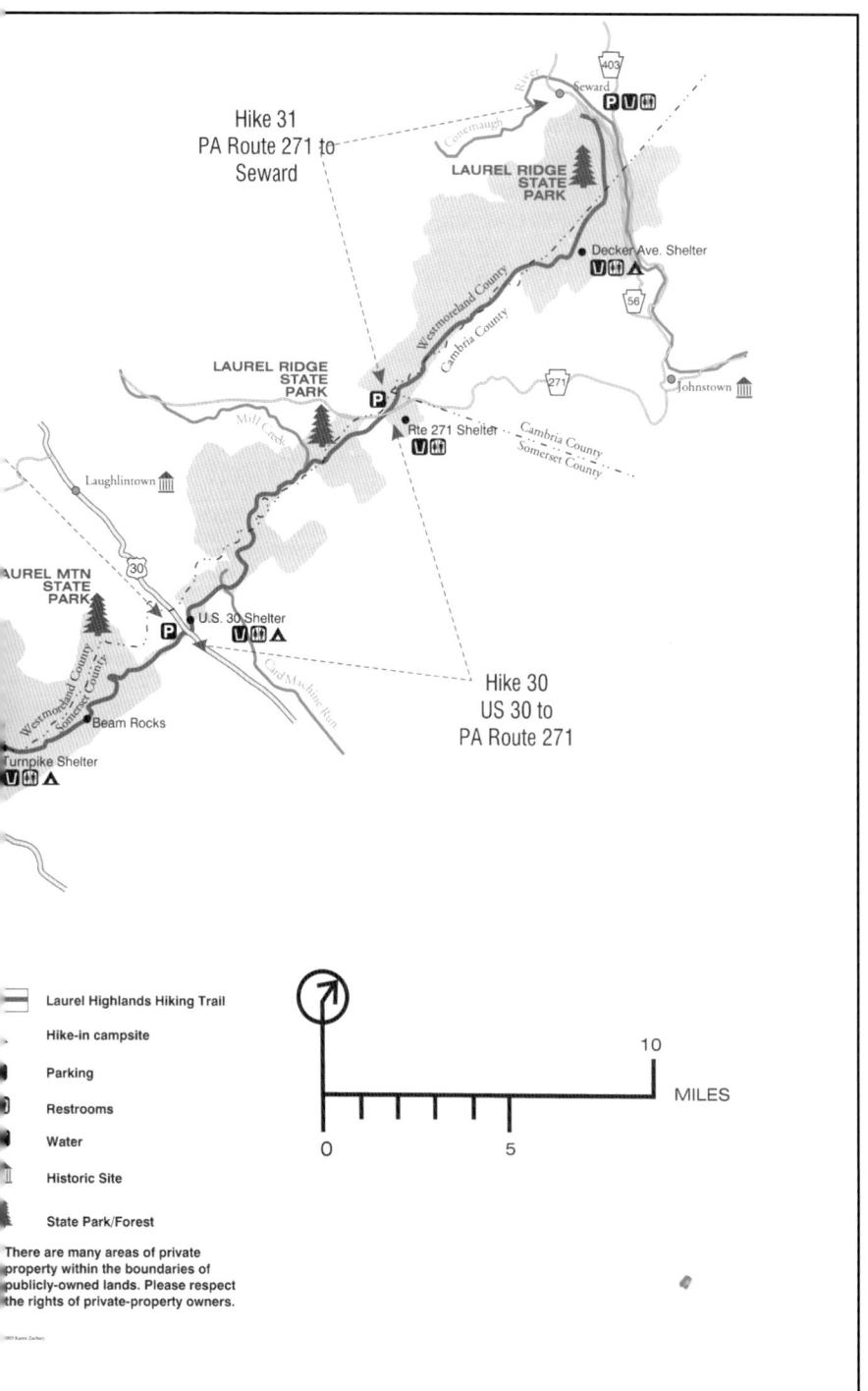

Hike 31
PA Route 271 to
Seward

403

Seward

LAUREL RIDGE
STATE
PARK

Conemaugh River

Decker Ave. Shelter

56

LAUREL RIDGE
STATE
PARK

Westmoreland County

Cambria County

271

Johnstown

Rte 271 Shelter

Mill Creek

Cambria County
Somerset County

Laughlintown

LAUREL MTN
STATE
PARK

30

U.S. 30 Shelter

Bird Machine Run

Hike 30
US 30 to
PA Route 271

Westmoreland County
Somerset County

Beam Rocks

Turnpike Shelter

Laurel Highlands Hiking Trail

Hike-in campsite

Parking

Restrooms

Water

Historic Site

State Park/Forest

There are many areas of private
property within the boundaries of
publicly-owned lands. Please respect
the rights of private-property owners.

10

MILES

0   5

Hike 27
Along the Laurel Highlands Hiking Trail
Ohiopyle to Route 653

Leaving the banks of the Youghiogheny River, the yellow-blazes of the Laurel Highlands Hiking Trail climb nine miles in stages from 1,200 feet to almost 2,800 feet. The second half of the section is gentle with the elevation hovering near 2,400 feet. The trail is well built, but rocky in places—a sturdy hiking shoe is a good choice here.

TRIP PLANNER

Start: Ohiopyle.
End: Route 653.
Miles: 19.0
Points of Interest: Ohiopyle; Laurel Ridge State Park Visitor Center.
Parking: Ohiopyle (0.0 mi.); Maple Summit Road (11.4 mi.);
Laurel Ridge State Park office (overnight permits, 19.0 mi.).
Water: Ohiopyle; Ohiopyle Shelter; Route 653 Shelter.
Restroom or Privy: Ohiopyle; Ohiopyle Shelter; Route 653 Shelter.
Provisions: Ohiopyle.
Camping: Ohiopyle Shelter; Route 653 Shelter. All shelters and campsites on the LHHT must be reserved in advance. A fee is required.

HIKE DATA

0.0 Ohiopyle. The depot houses restrooms and a visitor center. The store, B&Bs, hotel and outfitters are all within a few blocks.

0.2 Laurel Highlands Hiking Trail. Turn onto the yellow-blazed path. The trail is marked with mileposts. Except for the few miles at either end, the grades are gentle. It is open only to hikers.

6.5 Ohiopyle Shelter.

11.4 Maple Summit Road.

18.7 Route 653 Shelter.

19.0 Route 653.

EXPLORE THE TRAIL CORRIDOR

Ohiopyle. This little place is a major hub for recreation. It is most famous for whitewater rafting, but there is also a network of short trails. It's a memorable spot for fishing, too. Cross country skiing and snowshoeing offer the best way to solitude in the woods in winter. Just a few miles north on Route 381 is Fallingwater, the famous home built by Frank Lloyd Wright.

Laurel Highlands Hiking Trail. The LHHT is one of Pennsylvania's premiere hiking trails. It's especially fine for beginning backpackers: there are long stretches of level terrain and shelters spaced within easy walking distances. On this hike, the positions of the shelters on this trail make this segment an ideal two-day backpack. The first day covers less than seven miles, but tackles much of the climbing. The second day has one tough mile.

Hike 28
Along the Laurel Highlands Hiking Trail
Route 653 to Route 31

This section is a pleasant ridge top walk with expansive views. Early on the trail passes through house-size boulders before climbing gently to 2,994 feet, the highest point on the Potomac Heritage Trail. This is the most open section of Laurel Ridge. The trail crosses several ski slopes and open areas of the Seven Springs Ski Resort. The remnants of a tree farm provide a different look as the trail eases down to Route 31.

TRIP PLANNER

Start: Route 653.
End: Route 31.
Miles: 12.0
Points of Interest: Laurel Run Overlook; Seven Springs area.
Parking: Route 653 (0.0 mi.); Route 31 (12.0 mi.).
Water: Grindle Ridge Shelter.
Restroom or Privy: Grindle Ridge Shelter.
Provisions: None.
Camping: Grindle Ridge Shelter.

HIKE DATA

0.0   Route 653.
2.5   Laurel Run Overlook.
5.4   Grindle Ridge Shelter.
7.5   Seven Springs Resort. The Laurel Highlands Hiking Trail cuts right through a ski resort here. The open ski slopes offer wide open views.
8.0   Highest point on PHT, 2,994 feet.
12.0 Route 31.

EXPLORING THE TRAIL CORRIDOR

Seven Springs Mountain Resort. Due to its elevation this area is often encased in fog. The mist offers an opportunity to listen and get close to wildlife. Even if it is clear, you can stop and sit awhile along the edge of one of the ski slopes and see what flies by.

Hike 29
Along the Laurel Highlands Hiking Trail
Route 31 to Route 30

The scenery on this hike offers one delight after another. Probably the most scenic built structure is the metal bridge that carries the PHT over the Pennsylvania Turnpike.

TRIP PLANNER

Start: Route 31.
End: Route 30.
Miles: 15.0
Points of Interest: Pennsylvania Turnpike Bridge; Beam Rocks.
Parking: Route 31 (0.0 mi.); Route 30 (15.0 mi.).
Water: Route 31 lot; Route 31 Shelter; Turnpike Shelter; Route 30 parking lot.
Restroom or Privy: Route 31 Shelter; Turnpike Shelter.
Provisions: None.
Camping: Route 31 Shelter; Turnpike Shelter.

HIKE DATA

0.0   Route 31.
1.7   Route 31 Shelter.
6.0   Pennsylvania Turnpike Bridge. This massive iron bridge shows how serious the state was about getting this trail built.
7.4   Turnpike Shelter.
10.2 Beam Rocks.
15.0 Route 30.

EXPLORING THE PHT

Pennsylvania Turnpike Bridge. Take a few minutes to examine this massive structure. This is a fine example of Pennsylvania's commitment to foot trails.

Beam Rocks. There are many pinnacles and crevices to explore in this area of jumbled boulders. A blue blazed trail leads to the area. There are also three other marked side trails in the area which are worth a visit.

Hike 30
Along the Laurel Highlands Hiking Trail
Route 30 to Route 271

The Laurel Highlands Hiking Trail follows a gentle path high above the isolated valley of Mill Creek. The views here to the northwest of the trail are especially nice during the winter months. Close to Route 271, the trail passes through a series of rock formations worthy of exploration. Note that the Route 271 shelter is about 0.7 miles off the trail near the parking area.

TRIP PLANNER

Start: Route 30.
End: Route 271.
Miles: 11.7 (The section is only 11.0 miles excluding a visit to the shelter or parking lot).
Points of Interest: Card Machine Run; Mill Creek Valley; rock formations.
Parking: Route 30 (0.0 mi.); Route 271 (11.7 mi.).
Water: Route 30; Route 30 Shelter; Route 271 Shelter; Route 271.
Restroom or Privy: Route 30 Shelter; Route 271 Shelter.
Provisions: None.
Camping: Route 30 Shelter; Route 271 Shelter.

HIKE DATA

0.0   Route 30.
0.7   Route 30 Shelter.
2.2   Card Machine Run. There is a wonderful bog and spring here.
4.7   Mill Creek Valley.
10.2   Rock formations.
11.0   Route 271 crossing of Laurel Highlands Trail.
11.6   Route 271 Shelter (via side trail).
11.7   Route 271 parking lot (via side trail).

EXPLORING THE TRAIL CORRIDOR

Laughlintown, Pennsylvania. This is a village full of history. The Compass Inn Museum dates to 1799 and is listed on the National Register of Historic Places. The Inn was a stagecoach stop, 1820-1862, on the route which later became Route 30.

Hike 31
Along the Laurel Highlands Hiking Trail
Route 271 to Seward

This segment marks the end of the Laurel Highlands Hiking Trail and the conclusion of a magnificent journey of some 450 miles from Point Lookout in southern Maryland. There are spectacular views of the Conemaugh River Gorge to the north. Johnstown is to the east. The going is easy throughout, and culminates in a five-mile descent to Seward. The trail passes an old stone quarry and the remains of an incline plane. Both were used to gather materials for the construction of a railroad bridge in Johnstown. The bridge was said to be the site of many deaths during the Johnstown Flood of 1889, when buildings and debris piled against it. The incline plane was in use until 1930; the bridge still stands.

TRIP PLANNER
Start: Route 271.
End: Seward.
Miles: 13.3
Points of Interest: Conemaugh Gorge; Seward.
Parking: Route 271 (0.0 mi.); Seward (13.3 mi.).
Water: Route 271; Decker Avenue Shelter; Seward.
Restroom or Privy: Route 271; Decker Avenue Shelter; Seward.
Provisions: Seward, one mile from the terminus of the LHHT. To reach Seward, turn right on the road at end of the trail, and follow it to Route 56 on the Conemaugh River. Turn left to Seward.
Camping: Decker Avenue Shelter.

HIKE DATA
0.0   Route 271. Mileages in this section are counted from the trail crossing. If you walk from the parking area add 0.7 miles to all distances.
1.9   Cross Peak.
8.0   Side trail to Decker Shelter (0.3 miles).
8.7   Picnic area and lookout tower, east of trail.
11.6 Old quarry site.
13.3 Seward, northern terminus of the LHHT.

EXPLORE THE TRAIL CORRIDOR
Johnstown. Just east of trail's end. The Johnstown Flood Museum recounts the horrific events of 1889. Also, there is an active incline plane railway here. It was built in 1891 as a way to get people to higher ground during floods and to help develop the hillside.

Conemaugh Gorge. The ill-fated Pennsylvania Canal passed by here headed for Pittsburgh. It was an amazing achievement consisting of 277 miles of canal and 177 locks. There were 118 miles of railroad. It was completed from Philadelphia to Pittsburgh in 1829, but by 1864 it was no longer in use, outpaced by the railroads. Today, Conemaugh Valley Conservancy (CVC) is working to open trails in the Conemaugh Gorge. The trail system features four stone-arch bridges built in 1907. Eventually these trails and others will be linked to form a Pittsburgh to Harrisburg Greenway along the canal's former route. To find out about the trail's progress visit the conservancy website.

RESOURCES
Laurel Ridge State Park
(LHHT overnight permits)
(724) 455-3744
www.dcnr.state.pa.us/stateparks

Ohiopyle State Park
(724) 329-8591
www.dcnr.state.pa.us/stateparks

Conemaugh Valley Conservancy
www.conemaughvalleyconservancy.org.

Keystone Trails Association
www.kta-hike.org/laurel.htm

U.S. Army Corps of Engineers
(724) 459-7240

GREAT ALLEGHENY PASSAGE: OHIOPYLE TO PITTSBURGH

In the eastern U.S., there are few places that offer a casual hiker such immediate access to magnificent mountaintop vistas. Few trails offer so many miles with so few road crossings. The Great Allegheny Passage is expected to connect with the C&O Canal Towpath in Cumberland by late 2006, making the east-west connection envisioned by the canal's builders but never realized.

The Ohiopyle to Pittsburgh segments of the Passage are a "connecting route" to the Potomac Heritage National Scenic Trail. In hiking terms, it means if you're hiking the entire PHT, you have a decision to make when you reach Ohiopyle. For a ridgetop backpacking experience, climb Laurel Ridge and follow the Laurel Highlands Hiking Trail (see Hikes 27 to 31). To go "through the mountains, not over them," as the GAP's boosters say, walk along the Youghiogheny River toward the Forks of the Ohio in Pittsburgh.

All the maps you will need to navigate your way can be found on the website of the Allegheny Trail Alliance, www.atatrail.org. The website, like the ATA, is a terrific resource.

Hike 32
Along the Great Allegheny Passage
Ohiopyle to Connellsville

This remote section of the Great Allegheny Passage leaves town across a bridge over the Youghiogheny River and immediately enters dark woods. Just up trail, you cross a spectacular railroad trestle over another bend in the river. Side trails head to the campground here. Within a few miles you pass a trail junction for the Kaintuck Trail. North of here, there is unbroken solitude all the way to Greene Junction at the edge of Connellsville. There the trail crosses the valley on a 731-foot trestle. Minutes later a 746-foot monster brings the trail into Connellsville proper.

This is a notable spot on the GAP, where the route leaves the Western Maryland Railroad corridor which has been part of or adjacent to the route since Fort Frederick, Md. Through town the trail follows a pedestrian walkway along Third Street past Crawford Avenue, Route 711 and on to the end of the section at a parking lot in Riverfront Park.

TRIP PLANNER

Start: Ohiopyle.
End: Connellsville.
Miles: 17.0
Points of Interest: Ohiopyle; Kaintuck Trail; Bruner Run, Sheepskin Trail; Connellsville.
Parking: Ohiopyle (0.0 mi.); Connellsville (17.0 mi.).
Water: Ohiopyle; Connellsville.
Restroom or Privy: Ohiopyle; Connellsville.
Provisions: Ohiopyle; Connellsville.
Camping: Ohiopyle State Park.

HIKE DATA

0.0 Ohiopyle. The green painted depot serves as a combination restroom and visitor center. Cross the bridge and begin contemplating a Primanti's sandwich—it's a Pittsburgh thing that piles French fries and coleslaw in a sandwich for one-handed eating at the wheel of a truck.

0.6 State Park Campsites. Turn right up the hill just after you cross the second trestle.

3.3 Kaintuck Trail. The path leads to a series of trails in the Forbes State Forest.

6.6 Cross pipeline.

15.1 Cross trestle. The abandoned grade below is the proposed Sheepskin Trail.

15.4 Cross trestle.

16.6 Join Third Avenue.

16.8 Cross Crawford Avenue in Connellsville. Most services are within a few blocks including Amtrak, B&Bs, restaurants and shops. Motels are a bit further.

17.0 Riverfront Park. From Riverfront Park pass under Route 119 and climb the ramp to continue north on the old Pittsburgh & Lake Erie grade. If you see a stone milepost 58 (signifying the number of miles to Pittsburgh), then you're in the right place.

EXPLORING THE PHT

Ohiopyle. This little town in a park is a bit of a fantasy come true. Take the natural beauty and outdoor recreation of the state park, mix several small businesses to provide services and hospitality, add in a cappuccino and sip. Ohiopyle is a place that many park-town partnerships aspire to be, but few realize. Perhaps most famous for whitewater rafting, there is a network of short trails, bicycling and fishing. Cross-country skiing and snowshoeing offer the best ways to solitude in the woods in winter. Late afternoons are special. People of all ages lounge and wander about town—all still aglow after some outdoor adventure. And the Great Allegheny Passage is the main thoroughfare. Just a few miles north on Route 381 is Fallingwater, the famous home built by Frank Lloyd Wright.

Kaintuck Trail. This trail links to a series of foot trails in the Forbes State Forest. The West Virginia line is 38 miles away, then it's just a short jog to the 330-mile Allegheny Trail, which can be followed south to the Appalachian Trail near Pearisburg, Virginia.

Sheepskin Trail. This trail, still in development, will run 32 miles from Point Marion, Pennsylvania, to Connellsville, Pennsylvania. The line features a tunnel near the village of Outcrop. When complete, it will link the PHT to the Mon River Trail in West Virginia.

Connellsville. This town was at one time a colonial outpost—it's true, George Washington slept here. Later, it became a coal and railroad hub. Today it is known for Italian food and very friendly folks. Amtrak is positioned here for short trips either north to Pittsburgh or south to Cumberland. If you enjoy industrial history, this is a great place to spend time. There are also a number of grand churches here, as well as a library built by Andrew Carnegie.

Hike 33
Along the Great Allegheny Passage
Connellsville to Perryopolis

Once you leave town the trail regains the river and heads north. Five miles up the line note Dawson across the river. From here to Perryopolis, just enjoy the quiet and solitude. Early in the 20th century there were some 40,000 coke ovens in Fayette County alone, lighting the Youghiogheny River Corridor night and day. Contemplating this much industry and its bustle along this now solitary stretch, the day seems quieter still.

TRIP PLANNER

Start: Connellsville.
End: Perryopolis.
Miles: 12.8
Points of Interest: Connellsville; Dawson; Perryopolis.
Parking: Connellsville (0.0 mi.): Dawson (5.2 mi.); Perryopolis (12.8 mi.).
Water: Connellsville; Riverfront Park.
Restroom or Privy: Connellsville; Riverfront Park;
    Round Bottom Campground
Provisions: Connellsville; Adelaide: Dawson; Perryopolis.
Camping: Round Bottom Campground; Rivers Edge in Adelaide.

HIKE DATA

0.0   Connellsville. From Riverfront Park, pass under Route 119 and climb the ramp to continue north on the old Pittsburgh & Lake Erie grade. Look for your stone milepost 58, signifying the number of miles to Pittsburgh.

2.9   Rivers Edge Family Campground.

5.2   Dawson. To reach town, climb to bridge and cross river.

10.3   Round Bottom Campground. There is a privy, but no water here. Plan accordingly.

12.8   Perryopolis. Climb to the road that crosses above the trail, turn left and continue 1.5 miles to town. The tunnel and trestle you see here were filmed for a scene in the movie *Silence of the Lambs*.

EXPLORING THE PHT
Connellsville. See Hike 32 on page 94.
Dawson. Cross the river and enjoy the fine Victorian architecture. Today, only 500 folks live here, but it was once a hub of coal mining activity. Outstanding structures include the bank building and the Philip G. Cochran Memorial United Methodist Church, which dates to 1900 and boasts Tiffany windows.

Perryopolis. This is an enjoyable place to visit, if a little harder to get to. Your tour starts with the tunnel and trestle that cross the trail here. They were built in 1900 for the four-mile long Washington Run Railroad. Today they carry a road. A careful trip through the tunnel and across the river is a must. Back on the west side, pass through the tunnel again and climb the hill to town. You'll find an old style town square, a drugstore with a soda fountain, a blacksmith shop plus a gristmill and distillery open for tours.

Hike 34
Along the Great Allegheny Passage
Perryopolis to West Newton

This segment passes ruins associated with the coal mining that made this area famous. Stop and check out the remains and try to imagine what it was like to work underground for a living. Now that the coal is gone, towns like Smithton cling to life. For the rail fan, West Newton is a fine place for photos. Trains come right through town, barely clearing old buildings.

TRIP PLANNER
Start: Perryopolis.
End: West Newton.
Miles: 12.0
Points of Interest: Perryopolis; Whitsett: Banning #1 Mine; Smithton; West Newton.
Parking: Perryopolis (0.0 mi.); Whitsett (1.7 mi.); Smithton (6.0 mi.); Cedar Creek Park (8.5 mi.); West Newton (12.0 mi.).
Water: Cedar Creek Park, West Newton.
Restroom or Privy: Whitsett, Smithton, Cedar Creek Park, West Newton.
Provisions: Perryopolis; Cedar Creek Park; West Newton.
Camping: Cedar Creek Park Boater and Biker Campground.

HIKE DATA
0.0   Perryopolis. The town is 1.5 miles uphill to left.
1.7   Whitsett. This former company town is now a National Historic Landmark.
3.7   Banning Trestle.
3.8   Banning #1 Mine.
6.0   Smithton.
8.5   Cedar Creek Park. There is a snack bar and picnic area here.
12.0   West Newton. The headquarters of the Regional Trail Corporation, developer and maintainer of the Youghiogheny River Trail section

of the Great Allegheny Passage as well as other nearby trails, is located in the lower office beneath the Rite Aid store. Maps, T-shirts and trail accessories are available.

EXPLORING THE PHT
Perryopolis. See Hike 31 on page 92.
West Newton. There are lots of shops, a bike shop, and restaurants here as well as several B&Bs. The iron bridge crossing the river is vintage early 20th century. The now-closed radiator factory was once a paper mill, but the water here contained too much acid, so the mill moved to Markleton (See Hike 25 on page 80).

Hike 35
Along the Great Allegheny Passage
West Newton to McKeesport
Heading north, you are passing the remains of many mines—most will go unnoticed. The village of Industry is quiet now, but when the mines and coke ovens were running it lived up to its name. Further on you will pass Buena Vista and Boston. The trail now crosses the Yough at Boston and follows the east side of the river to McKees Point Marina and the end of the section.

TRIP PLANNER
Start: West Newton.
End: McKeesport.
Miles: 18.7 Miles
Points of Interest: West Newton; Industry; Buena Vista; Dravo Cemetery; Boston; Dead Man's Hollow Wildlife Preserve; McKeesport.
Parking: West Newton (0.0 mi.); Sutersville (3.9 mi.); Buena Vista (6.9 mi.); Boston (14.2 mi.); Iowa Street (17.1 mi.); McKees Point Park (18.7 mi.).
Water: Dravo Cemetery. Ask at stores in West Newton, Sutersville and Boston; McKeesport.
Restroom or Privy: West Newton; Collinsburg; Sutersville; Industry; Dravo Cemetery; Greenock; Boston.
Provisions: West Newton; Sutersville; Buena Vista; Boston; McKeesport.
Camping: Dravo Cemetery.

HIKE DATA
0.0   West Newton. Headquarters for the Regional Trail Corporation is in the lower office beneath the Rite Aid Store. It is located one block left of trail when you hit the main street. Maps and other trail

information are available here. T-shirts and trail accessories are for sale.

0.3 Saint Paul AME Church, built in 1880.

3.9 Sutersville.

5.4 Industry. Does this mean the people here that work hard are "industrious Industrians"?

6.9 Buena Vista.

8.5 Dravo Cemetery. Veterans from the Civil War and the War of 1812 are buried here. Camping is permitted and there is a well for water.

14.2 Boston Bridge.

14.3 Logan's Run; then railroad marker 19.

14.8 Enter Dead Man's Hollow Preserve.

14.9 Active railroad tracks begin to right of trail.

15.1 Pass entrance to Dead Man's Hollow Trails.

15.2 Leave grade; bear left and climb Durabond Bypass trail.

15.5 Pass junction of paved trails and go straight.

15.9 Bypass ends, join River Road; turn left.

16.8 Pass Glenn Avenue.

16.9 Bear left up ramp and reach 15th Street Bridge; turn right to cross the Youghiogheny River.

17.1 Bridge ends. Turn left, and enter McKeesport on trail.

17.3 Cross 13th Street.

17.4 Cross 12th Street.

17.5 Cross 11th Street.

17.6 Trail ends. Turn left, cross Market Street at Isbir Manor Apartments. Join Saunders Street. Pass through bollards, where trail resumes.

17.8 Reach the traffic circle. Ignoring walkways to the left, go straight on Water Street. Pass through bollards. The marina is on your left.

18 Yough River Trail section of the Great Allegheny Passage ends.

EXPLORING THE PHT
West Newton. See Hike 34 on page 98.
Dead Man's Hollow. This wonderful area is a reclaimed industrial site. It includes 2.5 miles of hiking trails. To reach the site follow the trail under the Boston Bridge and continue on the closed portion 1.2 miles to the preserve.

McKeesport. Many mills and interesting old buildings line the route. The spectacular railroad trestle across the Monongahela River is part of the Union Railroad. Planners hope to include it in the final alignment of the trail. This is also the gateway to the "Steel Heritage Trail" which the PHT will follow to the three rivers in Pittsburgh.

Montour Trail. This starts just a few miles west of Boston at the village of Clairton. The trail runs 52 miles to Coraopolis, north of Pittsburgh. Highlights include three tunnels and a spectacular trestle. Just yards from the terminus at Coraopolis, a city bus will bring you back to Pittsburgh.

Photo by Paul g. Weigman

Hike 36
Along the Great Allegheny Passage
McKeesport to Pittsburgh

When complete the Steel Valley Trail highlights will include spectacular bridges, old steel mills, including the famous Homestead Works, and a dramatic walk along the Monongahela River. The trail will end at Point State Park in Pittsburgh where the three rivers meet: the Allegheny, Monongahela and Ohio. This was to be the terminus of the Chesapeake & Ohio Canal, and the reason the canal is named the C&O rather than the Chesapeake to Cumberland. For now, sidewalks can be followed along most of the route. Approximately three miles are completed in the Waterfront development at Homestead as well as five miles along the Monongahela River from Station Square to Hayes. This section is a "one way" trail because it ends at a barricade in Hayes at an active railroad. Call numbers on page 104 for updates.

TRIP PLANNER

Start: McKeesport.

End: Pittsburgh.

Miles: Approximately 18.0

Points of Interest: McKeesport; Homestead Works; Kennywood Park; Point State Park; Pittsburgh.

Parking: McKeesport (0.0 mi.); Pittsburgh (18.0 mi.).

Water: McKeesport; Homestead; Point State Park; Pittsburgh.

Restrooms: Point State Park.

Provisions: McKeesport; Homestead; Pittsburgh.

HIKE DATA

0.0   Strawberry Street. Begin Steel Valley Heritage Trail section of the Great Allegheny Passage.

0.1   Market Street. Turn left. Then reach Lysle Boulevard. Turn right.

1.52   Bear right onto entrance ramp for McKeesport-Duquesne Bridge, built in 1928. Follow signs to Duquesne. Where ramp splits, bear left.

1.82   Bear right onto sidewalk and cross McKeesport-Duquesne Bridge. Cross on north side.

2.3   Bridge ends. Join Route 837. Turn right and follow shoulder

2.6   Cross to left side of road at traffic light. *Note: Changes in shoulders and sidewalks through the following passage will require crossing Route 837 a number of times.*

3.6   Climb hill on road.

3.7   Cross railroad on bridge.

4.7   Pass Kennywood Amusement Park.

6.2   Road splits. Follow Route 837 right.

6.7   East Waterfront Drive. Turn right at traffic light. Follow sidewalk.

7.5   Junction with paved trail that bears right behind townhouses along the Monongahela River.

8.6   Trail ends. Turn left and follow sidewalk towards shopping center.

8.7   Reach suspension bridge over the road and climb the steps, but do not cross. Instead bear right down the ramp to the sidewalk, following the road which the bridge crossed.

9.1   Reach Sandcastle Road. Turn left.

9.2   Pass five smokestacks from the Homestead Works.

9.3   Climb hill and reach the 1936 Homestead Grays Bridge. Turn right and follow walkway.

9.4   Rejoin Route 837, 8th Avenue. Turn right. Enter Homestead.

10.7 Reach stairway on right side of the road. Descend steps under Glenwood Bridge overpass. Walk under the overpass and go straight.

10.8 Baldwin Street. Turn right.

10.9 Join service road under Glenwood Bridge along railroad tracks. Use caution—tracks are active.

11.1 Join paved Three Rivers Heritage Trail section of the Great Allegheny Passage.

14.5 Pass Hot Metal Bridges on right. The trail will someday cross one of the bridges to link up with the Eliza Furnace Trail. Continue straight ahead on trail.

16.1 Trail segment ends. Turn left on South 9th Street. Cross railroad—active, use caution.

16.2 Bingham Street. Turn right.

16.5 South 4th Street. Turn left.

16.6 McKean Street. Turn right.

16.7 South 2nd Street. Turn right.

16.8 Rejoin trail. Turn left.

17.1 Smithfield Street Bridge. Pass under bridge through pedestrian tunnel, then climb steps to walkway. Turn left. Cross bridge.

17.3 Turn left on paved trail. Soon pass under elevated road through parking lot next to river.

18.0 Point State Park and the Forks of the Ohio.

EXPLORE THE PHT CORRIDOR.

McKeesport. See Hike 35 on page 99.

Homestead. The giant mill across the river, the Carrie Furnaces, was part of Andrew Carnegie's Homestead Works. It operated from the 1890s to the 1980s. It was the last steam-driven rolling mill, and is being restored as part of a museum complex. This area was also home to the Homestead Grays of the Negro National League. Led by the mighty Josh Gibson, the Grays once won eight pennants in nine seasons.

Point State Park. This is the point where the Allegheny and Monongahela rivers come together to form the Ohio. The restored Fort Pitt blockhouse and museum provide an interpretive history of the area. This is the western most terminus of the Potomac Heritage National Scenic Trail.

Pittsburgh. There is no limit on the possibilities here. For walkers, the town is a true hub. Nearby trails include the Montour, Eliza Furnace, South Shore, and the Three Rivers Heritage. Take time to enjoy a variety of historic bridges in the heart of town and a Primanti trucker sandwich in the Strip District.

Resources
Allegheny Trail Alliance.

Rather than list every contact for trail-related services from Ohiopyle to Pittsburgh, we recommend visiting the ATA website. It has the most comprehensive array of trail and travel information you will find.

RESOURCES
Allegheny Trail Alliance
www.atatrail.org.
(888) ATA-Bike

Amtrak
(800) 872-7245

Ohiopyle State Park
(800) 333-5661

Regional Trail Corporation
(724) 872-5586

Steel Valley Trail
www.steelvalleytrail.org

Photo by Paul g. Weigman

QUANTICO NATIONAL CEMETERY TO WHITES FERRY

Journalist Charles Kuralt wrote that if you want to see America, stay off the interstate highways. Traveling by car through Northern Virginia, keeping off big highways is not so easy to do. With the population growth and suburban design that define this region, planners have turned most thoroughfares into big roads and most big roads into really big roads. For visitors—even for residents—it's possible to think Northern Virginia consists only of highways, houses, and the commerce that serves car and home.

Traveling on foot you see Northern Virginia through an altogether different lens. In Prince William and Fairfax, you will see large tracts of public land, much of it along the Potomac River and its principal tributaries. There are towns and river communities built at a scale that showcases the landscape. Fairfax has preserved many of its stream valleys, enabling the creation of stream valley parks. In Loudoun, the Potomac Heritage Trail is being cobbled together foot by foot on and near the river—a remarkable feat given the county's status as one of the fastest growing counties in the U.S.

Hikers and paddlers are the only travelers able to experience the natural heritage of the Potomac with any continuity. Think of how the Potomac's character changes from Mason Neck to National Airport, then Roosevelt Island to Turkey Run, then Great Falls to Riverbend Park and northwest to Whites Ferry near Leesburg. Now imagine seeing those changes unfold in slow motion. In baseball, great hitters claim to see the rotating seams of a ball traveling at 90 miles per hour, and know by its motion where the ball will be as it arrives at the plate. The Potomac reveals itself frame by frame too. Only on foot or by paddle will you watch the river grow and appreciate what it carries to the Chesapeake Bay and the sea.

Nature is a star attraction of the hiking experience along the river in Northern Virginia, but history shares top billing. With names such as Washington, Mason, and Lee enshrined along the river, this is no surprise. But there also are the names of marines buried at Quantico National Battlefield, and farmers who scratched out a living in what is now Prince William Forest Park, and the millers and shippers who created the once bustling port at Occoquan. Their stories are revealed along the route.

This hiking guide to the Potomac Heritage Trail in Northern Virginia is divided into seven sections, or hikes. Together they create a continuous route for the Potomac Heritage Trail that a hiker could follow today. Some of these segments will eventually be part of a designated route for the trail. Those that follow sidewalks might later be re-routed onto off-road trails. Whether or not you want to hike the entire PHT corridor in Northern Virginia, you can use this guide to discover new parks and places, and to experience the breadth of the Potomac stories that together make up the river's heritage.

New trail segments are being developed in Northern Virginia that will improve the hiking experience. Before embarking on a long-distance hike, contact the local managing agency for maps and updates.

Hike 37
Quantico National Cemetery to Occoquan
This hike is divided into two sections, enabling hikers to walk the county in two days. The first section takes hikers through Quantico National Cemetery and Prince William Forest Park, then follows suburban side-

walks to the Julie J. Metz Wetlands Bank, just east of Route 1. The second section moves north on trails and sidewalks to the Town of Occoquan.

First section. The walk through Prince William begins in Quantico National Cemetery, following the access road. North of Joplin Road, the route enters Prince William Forest Park and traces stream valleys and wildlands through the length of the park. Beyond the park, this route follows suburban sidewalks en route to parks and wildlife areas along the Potomac River. The juxtaposition of the three experiences reveals a lot about conservation and community—the cemetery's solemn air, the park's rugged woodlands and historical sites, and the sidewalks' connection to the everyday. If, like most people, you don't plan to walk the entire county (at least not all at once!), consider walking this section north to south leaving time to linger in Quantico National Cemetery.

Second section. Many of the connections between parks and open space east of Route 1 are still in planning. This guide takes you as close as practical to such points of interest as Leesylvania State Park and Occoquan Bay National Wildlife Refuge, but in the interest of offering a continuous walking route does not go through them. Still, there is plenty of contact with water and trail. You can explore the points of interest along the way, moving by bicycle, boat or car in between.

TRIP PLANNER

Start: Quantico National Cemetery. The hike begins from the parking area off Russell Road south of the cemetery and just west of I-95. Traveling by car south on I-95, take Exit 148 and turn right on Russell Road. Take an immediate right onto a gravel road and park just outside the fence of Quantico Marine Corps Base.

Midpoint: Section 1 ends at Julia J. Metz Wetlands Bank (daytime trailhead parking available).

End: Town of Occoquan.

Miles: 17.7

Points of Interest: Quantico National Cemetery; Prince William Forest Park; Leesylvania State Park; Julie J. Metz Wetlands Bank; Veterans Park; Occoquan Bay National Wildlife Refuge; Town of Occoquan.

Parking: See Points of Interest; also, Virginia Rail Express stations on weekends or street parking along the way.

Water, Restrooms: Prince William Forest Park Visitor Center; Veterans Park; Occoquan; businesses along Route 1.

Provisions: Occoquan; businesses along Route 1.

Camping: Prince William Forest Park; group camping only at Leesylvania State Park.

HIKE DATA

0.0 The service road that climbs the hill east (right) of the trailhead leads into the cemetery. Climb the hill on the road, keeping right of the Marine base fence. Stay on the road! In about a quarter mile, you will pass two small office buildings, then further you will pass the cemetery support complex.

1.0 Enter cemetery grounds.

1.1 Pass through traffic circle and continue north on Quantico Drive (to the left as you approach the circle).

2.1 Turn right at traffic circle on Yorktown Boulevard.

2.4 Exit Quantico National Cemetery; turn right on Route 619, Joplin Road. Use caution; there is a lot of traffic on this road.

2.9 Turn left into Prince William Forest Park; entrance fee required. Continue past entrance station.

3.4 Turn left into Pine Grove picnic area (for visitor center, continue on park road another 150 yards). From the parking area, follow Laurel Trail west (left) loop.

3.9 Cross South Branch Quantico Creek. Turn left on white-blazed South Valley Trail. Follow the trail as it meanders along the creek, then crosses Scenic Drive twice.

5.4 Turn right on Taylor Farm Road. Over the next 1.5 miles, pass junctions with Meadows Trail, Old Back Top Road, and Scenic Drive (north of which the trail is called Burma Road).

6.9 Turn left on Pleasant Road and follow to Travel Trailer Village.

7.1 Exit Prince William Forest Park, turn right along roadway and cross Route 234, Dumfries Road, onto a dirt road at John F. Pattie Elementary School. Follow the school road into Anne Moncur Wall Park, then walk around ball fields. Turn right on Waterway Drive and follow the sidewalk.

7.6 Turn right on Northgate Drive, which becomes Beacon Drive.

8.4 Beacon Road ends at Cardinal Drive (there is pedestrian and bicycle access to Cardinal, but not vehicle access). Turn right and follow sidewalk.

9.6 Cross I-95; continue on Cardinal Drive.

10.4 Cross Route 1, Jefferson Davis Highway. End of first section. Future plans for the Potomac Heritage Trail include a route through the Julie J. Metz Wetlands Bank and Leesylvania State Park, which are reached by following Neabsco Road (see Exploring the PHT at the end of this hike). The Metz Wetlands is a logical midpoint for dividing this hike into two sections. The trailhead is about 0.4 miles ahead. For now, to continue on the PHT, turn left on Route 1 and follow the shoulder. The next quarter mile warrants caution. It is the only stretch on this hike that follows a major road without a sidewalk or trail, and there is a narrow bridge crossing over Neabsco Creek.

10.6 Turn right on Blackburn Road.

10.8 Follow path along right of tree line. You are following a sewer right of way—sounds odd but it's a nice walk away from the road, and the views of Neabsco Creek and the Metz Wetlands are very nice.

11.0 Just as Neabsco Creek widens, veer right and watch for trail to turn left into Rippon Landing Community Park. Follow nature trail north.

11.1 There are picnic tables and a pavilion. From the pavilion, return to sidewalk along Blackburn Road and turn right. Then, turn right on Rippon Boulevard. For the next 1.6 miles, follow sidewalks and, for a short section, the shoulder of the street through the community.

12.7 Farm Creek Drive and Virginia Rail Express Rippon Station. In the future, the trail will follow a wooded path east of the rail line, on land owned by the U.S. Fish & Wildlife Service. For now, turn left on Farm Creek Drive. The next mile of this interim route passes through an industrial park. There is ample space for pedestrians along the roadside. To the right, you can see the tree line of the future PHT route.

13.8 Turn right on Featherstone Road.

13.9 Cross the railroad track and bear left, following sidewalk, still on Featherstone Road.

14.2 Featherstone Road becomes Veterans Drive. Shortly after, enter Veterans Park. Follow the park road past tidal pond on left.

14.4 Turn right on nature path, which parallels park road north.

14.7 Rejoin park road. Turn right. The park office and parking lot are a hundred yards to the left. The park road ends in a cul de sac; the trail continues on a dirt path with the wildlife refuge on the right.

14.8 Pass through gate and continue on path toward industrial buildings.

14.9 Enter industrial park and turn right on Highams Court.

15.0 Turn left on Dawson Beach Road and follow through industrial area. (Woodbridge VRE station is to the north of the road.)

15.4 Cross Route 1, Jefferson Davis Highway, and follow sidewalk along Route 253, Occoquan Road.

15.9 Cross under I-95 and continue on sidewalk.

16.0 Cross Old Bridge Road.

17.7 Downtown Occoquan.

EXPLORING THE PHT

Quantico National Cemetery. The U.S. Marine Corps presence on the Potomac River at Quantico is as much a part of the river's heritage as

Colonial tobacco plantations. It seems only fitting that a pathway recognizing the heritage of the Nation's River should traverse a cemetery dedicated to the Marine Corps. It is a peaceful, beautiful landscape, lending itself to contemplation and offering an opportunity to express quiet gratitude to those whose service affords us the privilege—so rare in this world—to think of lofty ideas like conservation and heritage.

Prince William Forest Park. This 15,000-acre national park preserves one of the best examples of Piedmont forest in the nation. So close to Washington, D.C., there is no other place offering such abundant hiking, fishing, camping, cabins and wildlife watching. The park also tells the story of conservation in the U.S. Like most wildlands in the Eastern U.S., this place once was settled by farmers, miners and merchants. Beginning with the 17th century tobacco trade and ending with the Great Depression's subsistence farmers, the recorded human history has largely been supplanted by hardwood forest. Even the forest is an act of human intervention. During the 1930s, crews from the Civilian Conservation Corps reforested the land and built five cabin camps as a recreation respite for city dwellers. The suburbs of Washington, D.C. have now grown to the park's boundaries. Except for the occasional sounds of Marine Corp training, all remains quiet in the woods.

Julie J. Metz Wetlands Bank. We've all heard how important wetlands are to the health of waterways. Ever wondered how they really work? This is the first wetlands bank in Northern Virginia, designed and constructed to mitigate the loss of wetlands elsewhere. There are two miles of trails, interpretive signs and brochures describing the natural systems of wetlands. Plus, the views of the creek and wildlife will make you forget you're only a half mile from Route 1. The wetlands bank also provides a vital link to the PHT—a footbridge will one day cross to the northern shore of Neabsco Creek, linking to Blackburn Road and Rippon Landing Community Park. The site is named for Julie J. Metz, a scientist who led efforts to create federal wetlands banks.

Leesylvania State Park. This 508-acre park typifies the heritage experience along the PHT. It is part nature, part cultural history and part conservation story. Situated on a peninsula called Freestone Point, it is the birthplace of Light Horse Harry Lee, a Revolutionary War hero and the father of General Robert E. Lee, commander of the army of the Confederate States of America. It contains several miles of trails, stunning contact with the Potomac River and Neabsco and Powells creeks, history exhibits and remnants of centuries old structures. The park offers group camping by reservation.

Occoquan. Featured as the final destination along this hike, Occoquan is itself reason enough for a 17-mile walk. To the Dogue Indians, it was the "end of the water." This is likely a reference to the village's proximity to the end of tidewater at the falls above Occoquan. Standing on the village's pedestrian bridge over the Occoquan, it's easy to see why the Dogue called the river home. The river is navigable for small craft and large enough to provide a stable food source. It has the added advantage of being downright picturesque. In the mid-18th century, it boomed with milling operations utilizing the substantial fall of the river into tidewater. That combination of water power for milling and port access to the Potomac turned Occoquan into a vibrant economic center. All manner of goods and agricultural products left from Occoquan bound for ports along the eastern seaboard. Today, the town's history and charm are its principle assets. There are museums, galleries, eateries, and streets to stroll. You can even get a great cheese steak at Sports, just outside of town.

Rippon Lodge

Hike 38
Occoquan to Mount Vernon
This segment of the PHT corridor is still evolving. Laurel Hill Park, formerly Lorton penitentiary, provides an opportunity for a future PHT route. Although this segment requires several miles of roadside walking, the parks it visits are worth the effort. Among the jewels along the Potomac visited in this hike are Accotink Bay Wildlife Refuge and Mount Vernon.

TRIP PLANNER

Start: Footbridge over the Occoquan River in the Town of Occoquan.

End: Mount Vernon.

Miles: 11.4

Points of Interest: Town of Occoquan historic district; Occoquan Regional Park; Accotink Bay Wildlife Refuge; Grist Mill Park; Mount Vernon.

Parking, Water, Restrooms: Town of Occoquan; Occoquan Regional Park; Mason Neck West Area Park; Pohick Bay Regional Park; Gunston Hall Plantation; Meadowood Recreation Area; Accotink Bay Wildlife Refuge; Grist Mill Park; Mount Vernon.

Provisions: Occoquan, businesses along Route 1 near Fort Belvoir.

Camping: Pohick Bay Regional Park.

Lodging: Town of Occoquan.

HIKE DATA

0.0   Cross the footbridge from Occoquan and turn right onto blacktop road.

0.3   Ascend hill left and reach Route 123. Turn left and follow shoulder.

0.9   Cross Route 123 and enter Occoquan Regional Park.

1.0   Turn right at white-posts that mark entrance to nature trail and ascend into woods 100 yards to a rest stop with benches and amphitheater overlooking the Occoquan River and town.

1.3   Reach park access road; turn right and follow alongside park road. Follow blue-blazed trail past ball fields and into woods. Follow blue blazes.

2.0   Reach boat dry dock. Follow treeline left 50 yards to power line. Turn left and ascend.

2.2   Emerge from woods and cross field to landfill access road. Turn right.

2.3   Turn right on Route 611, Furnace Road. Pass under I-95.

2.5   Cross Route 1.

2.7   Turn left on Old Colchester Road.

3.3   Mason Neck West Area Park. Over the next three miles, the road is windy with little shoulder area, but generally sight lines are good. This section is not recommended for novice road walkers—this is merely the best connection at this time between Occoquan and Accotink Wildlife Refuge for those who want to walk a continuous route.

4.5   Cross Route 242, Gunston Road.

5.1   Pass through Lower Potomac Pollution Control Project area— primarily, wetlands and marshes and very pleasant walking despite lack of a roadside shoulder. Accotink Bay Wildlife Refuge is on the right. A potential trail alignment would route hikers through the refuge and a portion of Fort Belvoir outside the secure areas.

5.7 Turn right on Route 1.

8.0 Tulley Gate entrance to Fort Belvoir and Accotink Wildlife Refuge. Walking north with Fort Belvoir on your right, there are numerous opportunities to get away from the road, including an intermittent trail and the power line right-of-way.

8.8 Pass Woodlawn Stables on right.

9.0 Turn right on Route 235, Mount Vernon Memorial Highway. There is a sidewalk and intermittent trail from here to Grist Mill Park, 1.5 miles east of Route 1.

9.3 Washington Grist Mill.

10.5 Grist Mill Park. Follow the paved trail that east toward Mount Vernon.

11.4 Mount Vernon.

EXPLORING THE PHT

Town of Occoquan. See Hike 37 on page 106.

Occoquan Regional Park. This 400-acre park tries to offer a little bit to everyone, serving up everything from batting cages to boat ramps. But its main attraction for hikers are views of the Occoquan River from the wooded path above the river, the remains of a brick kiln and a curious graveyard about which little is known. Thought by some to be the resting place of a Selectman family (that was their name, not their position), it is not known whether the remains were moved to a new site, as outlined in the deed of sale to the Holt family, or whether they are buried there still. Or it may be the gravesite of a Hogue Indian chief, as described in a fascinating website called Cemeteries of Fairfax County. The PHT hike through the park described in this guide uses a portion of a self-guided, well-marked loop. For a relaxing sojourn, couple a hike here with a visit to the town of Occoquan.

Gunston Hall Plantation. The 500-acre heritage area was the home of George Mason, a Virginia patriot and a formative leader in American politics. One of the most influential thinkers in U.S. political history, Mason, because he shunned public life, is less known than his Commonwealth compatriots. Most of the preserved land on Mason Neck was part of the Mason estate. Gunston Hall's gardens and nature trail leading to the Potomac River are open to the public.

Pohick Bay Regional Park. Pohick Bay just might be the perfect place for hikers to trade in their boots for paddles. If you don't own a kayak, rent one here and take a lesson.

Mason Neck State Park. Surrounded by water and Mason Neck Wildlife Refuge, Mason Neck Park offers what few Potomac area waterfront parks do: both intimate contact with the water and a total emphasis on nature and solitude. The park also tells an inspiring conservation story. After bald eagles were sighted in the area in the mid 1960s, the Mason Neck Conservation Committee began advocating protection for the peninsula. The Nature Conservancy and the Commonwealth of Virginia teamed up for the purchase of the parcel, with assistance from federal grants. But efforts to protect the peninsula didn't end so quickly. Proposals for an airport, a highway, gas pipeline, landfill and sewer line were all resisted by Mason Neck Conservation Committee and the friends it recruited. Mason Neck State Park opened to the public in April 1985.

Accotink Wildlife Refuge. Located within the boundaries of Fort Belvoir, the refuge is managed by the U.S. Army. While this translates into the

uncommon experience of entering the area accompanied by assorted military vehicles, the refuge is all about wildlife and hiking. The trails are open to foot travel only—an increasing rarity in the Washington, D.C. region—and the only sounds coming from Accotink Bay are the winds and fowl. About the only way to improve upon the experience would be to establish a route for the Potomac Heritage Trail through the refuge so that it could be accessed by through-hikers and others without the need to rely on a car. Open year round, dawn to dusk.

Mount Vernon. Tours of the grounds here are given daily—free on February 22, George Washington's birthday. A souvenir shop and a restaurant make this a great place to spend the entire day.

Hike 39
Along the Mount Vernon Trail
Mount Vernon to Key Bridge

Beginning at the steps of Mount Vernon, this hike follows the Potomac River and the George Washington Parkway along the Mount Vernon Trail. More than 20 bridges are crossed, including two stretching more than 1,000 feet across vast marshlands. Near the 10-mile mark, the route passes through Old Town Alexandria on sidewalks. A number of side trails lead to historic sites along the way. An added bonus is that both ends of the section are served by public transportation and that the National Airport metro stop is right on the trail five miles south of Key Bridge.

TRIP PLANNER

Start: Mount Vernon.

End: Key Bridge.

Miles: 18.3

Points of Interest: Mount Vernon; Fort Hunt; Dyke Marsh; Jones Point; Old Town Alexandria; National Airport; Theodore Roosevelt Island; Arlington National Cemetery; Iwo Jima.

Parking: Mount Vernon (0.0 mi.); Riverside Park (1.2 mi.); Fort Hunt Park (2.8 mi.); Dyke Marsh (7.6 mi.); Daingerfield Island (12.3 mi.); Gravelly Point (15.0 mi.); LBJ Memorial Grove (16.1 mi.); Roosevelt Island (17.9 mi.).

Water, Restrooms: Mount Vernon; mile 1.9; Fort Hunt Park; Belle Haven Marina; Alexandria; Daingerfield Island; LBJ Memorial Grove; Columbia Island; Theodore Roosevelt Island (closed in winter); Rosslyn.

Provisions: Alexandria; Crystal City; Rosslyn.

Camping: None.

Lodging: Alexandria, Crystal City, Rosslyn.

HIKE DATA

0.0   Mount Vernon. Follow the parking lot to the trailhead.

0.2   Join Mount Vernon Trail.

1.1   Cross Little Hunting Creek.

1.9   Water fountain.

2.4   Fort Washington visible across the Potomac in Maryland.

2.8   Fort Hunt Park.

3.3   Waynewood Boulevard.

4.2   Collingwood Road.

4.7   Wellington Road.

5.1   West Boulevard Drive.

5.2   Join Alexandria Avenue. Turn left.

5.3   Northdown Road. Turn left.

5.5   Trail resumes.

6.2   Dyke Marsh.

6.8   Bridge across Dyke Marsh.

7.0   Bridge ends.

7.6   Belle Haven Marina. Dyke Marsh entrance road.

7.7   Jones Point. This was the southernmost point of the District of Columbia between 1790 and 1846.

8.7   South Street in Alexandria; turn right, join sidewalk.

8.9   South Royal Street; turn left and pass under the Woodrow Wilson Bridge, then turn right. Watch for detours here during bridge construction.

9.3   Trail resumes; turn left.

9.6   Battery Rodgers.

9.7   South Union Street; turn right.

9.8   Cameron Run Trail junction. The railroad tunnel on the left was built in 1856.

10.2   King Street.

10.4   Founders Park.

10.6   Pendleton Street; turn left and cross railroad tracks.

10.7   Trail resumes; turn right.

11.4   Bridge at power plant.

11.8   Junction with trail to Northern Alexandria.

12.3   Daingerfield Island.

12.9   Junction with Four Mile Run Trail.

13.1   National Airport.

13.6   Pass under Metro tracks.

15.0   Gravelly Point; cross airport flight path.

15.8   Pass under 14th Street Bridge.

16.1 Navy and Marine Memorial.

16.9 Trail to Arlington Cemetery.

17.0 Pass under Memorial Bridge.

17.6 Pass under Route 50.

17.9 Footbridge to Roosevelt Island.

18.1 Westbound PHT towards Cabin John Bridge.

18.3 Key Bridge. Rosslyn Metro is two blocks to the left. The connection via Key Bridge to the Maryland PHT is described in Hike 40.

EXPLORING THE PHT.

Mount Vernon. See Hike 38 on page 111.

Dyke Marsh. This area features 380 acres of tidal marsh, floodplain and swamp forest. There is a hiking trail here as well as opportunities to fish and paddle. This is the largest remaining tidal wetland in the Washington area.

Jones Point. A beautiful riverside setting complete with a lighthouse built in 1856. One of the original 40 District of Columbia boundary stones is here as well. When the District was a perfect square this was its southernmost point. Access may be limited during construction of the new bridge.

Old Town Alexandria. Wander the streets and enjoy a seemingly endless array of galleries, shops, bars and restaurants, or just walk the waterfront. This was once a bustling port and a center for shipbuilding. There was so much commerce that the Alexandria Canal was built to connect Virginia directly to the C&O Canal.

Theodore Roosevelt Island Park. A wild 91-acre tract purchased and named for Roosevelt in 1932. The island has had many owners, including the family of George Mason. The two-mile loop trail includes a half-mile boardwalk section.

Hike 40
Along the Potomac Heritage Trail
Theodore Roosevelt Island to Scotts Run Nature Preserve

This natural surface foot trail was the first trail to carry the name Potomac Heritage Trail. It begins at the parking area for Theodore Roosevelt Island. The route is fairly rugged, especially the first four miles to Chain Bridge. For long stretches the trail is narrow and close to the river, which in high water tends to wash out. After turning inland for awhile, the trail returns to the Potomac shoreline for a steep run up to Live Oak Drive at the Cabin John Bridge.

TRIP PLANNER

Start: Roosevelt Island.

End: Scotts Run Nature Preserve, Swinks Mill Road trailhead.

Miles: 10.8

Points of Interest: Roosevelt Island; Rosslyn; Fort Marcy; Turkey Run Park.

Parking: Roosevelt Island (0.0 mi.); Windy Run (1.8 mi. via side trail); Gulf Branch Nature Center (3.8 mi via 0.8 mile side trail); North Glebe Road (4.3 mi.); Fort Marcy (4.8 mi.); Turkey Run Park (7.5 mi. via 0.3 mile side trail).

Water: Roosevelt Island; Gulf Branch Nature Center; Turkey Run Park.

Restroom or Privy: Roosevelt Island; Turkey Run Park.

Provisions: Rosslyn.

Camping: None.

HIKE DATA

0.0   Roosevelt Island parking lot. Junction with paved Mount Vernon Trail

0.2   Pass under Key Bridge.

1.8   Windy Run Trail.

3.8   Trail to Gulf Branch Nature Center.

4.2   Chain Bridge. Access to the Maryland PHT across the river.

4.3   North Glebe Road.

4.8   Fort Marcy.

7.5   Trail to Turkey Run Park.

8.2   Turkey Run.

9.4   Dead Run.

9.9   Pass under Cabin John Bridge.

10.0 Live Oak Drive. Continue west toward woods.

10.2 Enter Scotts Run Nature Preserve at Langley Swim Club (no parking). Follow Woodland Trail, staying on trail at two junctions leading right.

10.5 Turn right on Loop Trail, then stay left as Woodland Trail continues to river. To visit river stay on Woodland Trail, then take River Trail back to Swinks Mill Road Trailhead.

10.6 Turn right at Woodland Trail.

10.8 Swinks Mill Road Trailhead parking.

EXPLORING THE PHT
Roosevelt Island. See Hike 39 on page 115.

Fort Marcy. This was one of the 67 forts that ringed Washington during the Civil War. Situated on Prospect Hill and completed in 1862, the fort measured 338 feet in diameter. The earth works are still in place. Originally named Fort Baldy Smith, it was renamed for Randolph Marcy the father-in-law of General George McClellan.

NOTE: Scotts Run to Great Falls Park. The short gap between Scotts Run and Great Falls Park currently offers no recommendable roadside walking route.

To pick up the trail at the next safe trailhead, park at the Difficult Run Trailhead on Georgetown Pike. Continue downstream another hundred yards to the access trail under Georgetown Pike. You can follow Difficult Run all the way to the Potomac River.

For a terrific day hike, explore Difficult Run. This natural surface trail offers views of Difficult Run gorge and close contact with the stream. There are moderate ascents, but few that are sustained. A truly fine hike! For information, see www.fairfaxtrails.org/maps.

Hike 41
Great Falls Park to Algonkian Regional Park

Important notes: This hike is included in anticipation of a bridge to be constructed over Sugarland Run in Loudoun County. The bridge is scheduled for construction in 2006 (just as this book went to press). Check the website of the Northern Virginia Regional Park Authority before your hike: www.nvrpa.org. Or call (703) 352- 5900. If the bridge is not in place, you can complete this section only by detouring to county roads. Even without the bridge, this hike is a fine out-and-back excursion.

Hiking north out of Riverbend in morning, it is possible to have the Potomac River entirely to yourself. There are few access points along the

trail, which eliminates a lot of traffic, and makes this segment one of the quietest along the PHT in the Washington, D.C. area.

The hike begins at Great Falls Visitor Center. Or you can join the hike at a convenient place along the River Trail in the park. The hike follows the River Trail north into Riverbend Park, then bends west with the river to follow trail lands of Northern Virginia Regional Park Authority and Fairfax County. In places, the trail passes over trail easements on private land—this means the property owner is allowing public access over their land to hikers. The best way to show your appreciation is to stay on the trail! In Loudoun County the trail passes through Lowes Island on a trail easement, then enters Algonkian Regional Park.

The trail remains in intimate contact with the river in what is, by and large, a leisurely hike. There are a few modest climbs over knobs and around streams.

TRIP PLANNER
Start: Great Falls Park Visitor Center.
End: Boat launch at Algonkian Regional Park.
Miles: 13.5
Points of Interest: Great Falls Park; Riverbend Park; Algonkian Regional Park.
Parking: Great Falls Park; Riverbend; Algonkian Regional Park.
Water, Restrooms: Great Falls Park Visitor Center; Riverbend Park Visitor Center; Algonkian Park office.
Provisions: Snacks are available at park concessions at Great Falls and Riverbend (ice cream and chips).
Camping: Cottages at Algonkian.

TRAIL DATA
0.0   Great Falls Visitor Center.
1.7   Riverbend Park Visitor Center.
3.3   Utility right-of-way.
5.0   Utility access road.
6.9   Lowes Island Golf Club.
9.5   Sugarland Run. A bridge is planned that will connect Algonkian with Lowes Island.
10.5   Algonkian Regional Park boat launch.

EXPLORING THE PHT
Riverbend Park. Located just north of Great Falls Park, Riverbend is often overlooked by the larger crowds seeking views of the water rushing over the fall line. This is fine with Riverbend's devotees, especially birders who quietly ply the woods with binoculars and cameras. The park's more than 400 acres are thickly forested, punctuated by meadows of native grasses. The setting, along with the park's position on the river, attracts an incredible variety of birds and wildlife—and a diverse array of people who enjoy watching them. The visitor center contains natural history exhibits,

a library and guidebooks. After a morning of walking, fishing or birding, there are picnic tables for enjoying lunch by the river.

Hike 42
Algonkian Regional Park to Whites Ferry

On this hike, the route leaves the Potomac River to follow local jogging and bicycle paths through Loudoun County neighborhoods, primarily along the county's network of parkways. It is an interim route available and accessible today, while Loudoun moves forward with planning more PHT trail segments along the Potomac.

Who will hike this entire segment in its current form? Hikers who want to complete the entire PHT, people who are curious about suburban parkway connectivity, and hearty souls who want to walk a goodly stretch of their county.

En route to Whites Ferry, the route visits two exceptional Potomac sites, Red Rock Wilderness Area and Balls Bluff. It crosses into Maryland at Whites Ferry—on the ferry, that is—and connects with the C&O Canal National Historical Park.

Red Rock and Balls Bluff are exceptional natural areas with immediate contact with the Potomac. Balls Bluff commemorates and interprets the Civil War battle fought there. Both offer the kind of immediate escape from hustle and bustle that the best urban and suburban parks provide.

The walks along the parkways are pleasant and, at times, scenic. Admittedly, people are unlikely to travel to the region merely to hike this segment through suburbia. Still, the parkways illustrate a moment in America's story, one in which mammoth-scale residential development gives rise to the realization of the parkway idea. Loudoun County is laced with new and planned parkways designed both to move people efficiently by car and enable them to travel leisurely on foot. While some of these boulevards are nothing more than sidewalk-lined suburban arteries, others uphold the ideal of the "park way," a green (or at least greenish) ribbon connecting communities.

TRIP PLANNER

Start: Algonkian Regional Park boat launch area.
End: Whites Ferry crossing of the Potomac River.
Miles: 14.0
Points of Interest: Algonkian Regional Park; Red Rock Wilderness Overlook Regional Park; Balls Bluff; Whites Ferry.
Parking: In addition to parking at each park along the way, most of the hike follows public roads that provide for temporary parking.

Water, Restrooms: Algonkian Regional Park. The lack of woodland "cover" along the parkways presents the biggest challenge of this hike!

Provisions: Whites Ferry store on Maryland shore.

Camping, Lodging: Cottages at Algonkian Park, Campsites one mile upriver and one mile downriver from Whites Ferry along the C&O Canal Towpath; B&Bs in Leesburg.

HIKE DATA

0.0 From the parking lot of the launch area walk toward the park entrance, following the park access road. Just beyond the parking area, turn right and continue on the park road. Golf course will be on your left.

0.7 Turn right on Cascades Parkway (you're still in the park).

0.8 Leave the park and continue on Cascades Parkway.

1.0 Turn right on Algonkian Parkway following trails and sidewalks.

3.4 Turn right on Winding Way, the last street before reaching the Route 7 overpass.

3.9 Turn left on Broad Run, then, in 75 yards, turn right on Route 7. Stay on the shoulder.

4.1   This is the one tricky spot on the hike. With traffic merging from the right, you need to cross the merge lane to reach the shoulder of Route 7. Continue on Route 7.

5.9   Turn right at Landsdowne Boulevard.

6.2   Turn left on Riverside Parkway. For the first 300 yards, stay on the shoulder, then follow trail and sidewalks.

7.2   Cross Belmont Road. Continue on Riverside Parkway.

7.8   Cross Goose Creek.

8.4   Turn right on River Creek Parkway. Follow trail and sidewalks.

9.2   Road turns left and becomes Edwards Ferry Road.

9.4   Red Rock Wilderness Overlook.

10.3   Turn right on Battlefield Parkway. Follow sidewalks and trails.

11.1   Balls Bluff Road. To reach Balls Bluff Regional Park, turn right and follow Balls Bluff Road 0.2 miles.

11.3   Turn right on Route 15. Follow shoulder.

13.0   Turn right on Whites Ferry Road. The first 200 yards are tight, but except when a ferry has just arrived on the Virginia shore, traffic is light. After the first 200 yards, sight lines are good.

13.8   Turn left at the bottom of the hill.

14.0   Whites Ferry crossing of the Potomac.

EXPLORING THE PHT

Algonkian Regional Park. This waterfront park is primarily known for its boat launch area, golf and picnicking. Cottages are available for overnight use.

Balls Bluff Regional Park. The park commemorates the October 21, 1861, Battle of Balls Bluff. The two sides met with roughly 1,700 troops apiece, but it ended in a rout, with Confederate soldiers capturing more than 500 Union prisoners as they fled into the Potomac River. An interpretive trail tells the battle's story. Balls Bluff National Cemetery also is on the grounds; 54 Union soldiers, all but one unknown, are buried here. There are no restrooms or services at this site.

Leesburg. An historic village with many places to eat and drink and sip coffee, Leesburg also is home to the Balch Library, one of the best local history libraries anywhere. Leesburg is popular with antiques hunters, but very welcoming to hikers in boots. Among the culinary treats are terrific barbecue at the Mighty Midget, Central American charcoal-broiled chicken, and a couple of fine delis—among these, Puccio's rules. There also are fine dining restaurants that pride themselves in serving up locally grown food and wine, and a wonderful, authentic diner.

Red Rock Wilderness Overlook. You can spend an hour or a day in this park enjoying the woods and views of the Potomac. The white-blazed

Pine Loop Trail is a 1.4 mile circuit that takes you down to the river and up to overlooks offering prospect of the water and the historic C&O Canal in Maryland. There are plentiful stream crossings—all over footbridges. Several connecting trails allow you to vary your hike with each visit or create shorter circuits. Near the parking area are the remains of 19th century outbuildings. Near the house, which is a private residence, are a restored smokehouse and icehouse. There are no restrooms or services.

RESOURCES
Accotink Wildlife Refuge
U.S. Army Garrison, Fort Belvoir
(703) 806-4007
Environmental Education Center: (703) 805-3972

Arlington County Department of Parks, Recreation & Community Resources
(703) 228-4747
www.co.arlington.va.us/prcr

Atlantic Kayak Company
Store, tours and classes
1201 North Royal Street
Alexandria, VA 22314
(703) 838-9072
www.atlantickayak.com

Fairfax County Park Authority
(703) 324-8702
http://www.co.fairfax.va.us/parks/

Fairfax Trails and Streams
www.fairfaxtrails.org

Fort Marcy Park
(703) 289-2500
www.nps.gov/gwmp/vapa/FtMarcy.htm

Friends of Prince William Forest Park
http://65.166.19.230/FPWFP/secure/Home.asp

George Washington Memorial Parkway
(703) 289-2500
www.nps.gov/gwmp

Great Falls Park
www.nps.gov/grfa

Gunston Hall Plantation
10709 Gusnton Road
Mason Neck, VA 22079
(703) 550-9220
www.gunstonhall.org

Leesylvania State Park
2001 Daniel K. Ludwig Dr.
Woodbridge, VA 22191-4504
(703) 670-0372
http://www.dcr.state.va.us/parks/leesylva.htm

Loudoun County Dept. of Parks, Recreation & Community Services
(703) 777-0343
www.loudoun.gov/prcs/home.htm

Mason Neck State Park
7301 High Point Road
Lorton, VA 22079-40101
(703) 550-0362
www.dcr.state.va.us/parks/masonnec.htm

Meadowood Special Recreation Management Area
Bureau of Land Management
10406 Gunston Road
Lorton, VA 22079
(703) 339-8009
www.es.blm.gov/lands/meadowood

Metro Transit Information
(202) 637-7000

Mount Vernon Trail
George Washington Memorial Parkway
(703) 289-2500
 www.nps.gov/gwmp

Mount Vernon
(703) 780-2000
www.mountvernon.org.

National Park Service, National Capital Region
www.nps.gov/ncro

Northern Virginia Regional Commission
The NVRC has published a map collection called Guide to
Recreation Trails in Northern Virginia.
(703) 642-0700
www.novaregion.org

Northern Virginia Regional Park Authority
5400 Ox Road
Fairfax Station, VA 22039
Phone: (703) 352-5900
www.nvrpa.org

Town of Occoquan
www.occoquan.com

Pohick Bay Regional Park
6501 Pohick Bay Drive
Lorton, VA
Camp Center: (703) 339-6104
http://www.nvrpa.org/pohickbay.html

Potomac Appalachian Trail Club
www.patc.net

Prince William County Chamber of Commerce
(703) 590-5000
www.prcgmcc.org

Prince William County Park Authority
(703) 792-7275
www.pwcparks.org/

Prince William Forest Park
18100 Park Headquarters Road
Triangle, VA 22172
(703) 221-4706
www.nps.gov/prwi

Riverbend Park
8700 Potomac Hills Street
Great Falls, VA 22066
(703) 759-3211

Quantico National Cemetery
www.cem.va.gov/nchp/quantico.htm

U.S. Fish & Wildlife Service
www.refuges.fws.gov

Veterans Memorial Park Center
14300 Featherstone Road
Woodbridge, VA 22191
(703) 491-2183
TTY (703) 491-6774

VIRGINIA'S NORTHERN NECK
A guide to hiking and walking destinations

Virginia's Northern Neck is the type of place travel writers are reluctant to describe in print—they want the place all to themselves. A few towns, lots of timber land, and hundreds of miles of shoreline incorporating coves and tidal creeks are the most visible characteristics viewed from car windows. At a slower pace travelers discover crab shacks and barbecue, nature preserves and parks, historical sites, fishing and all manner of outdoor pursuits.

Surrounded by the waters of the Potomac and Rappahannock rivers and the Chesapeake Bay, the neck is the eastern region of a peninsula stretching from Fredericksburg to Reedville and other points on the bay. While the Potomac often gets top billing among the region's waterways, the heritage of the Northern Neck is also tied to the Rappahannock and all the land and drainages between the two rivers. This hiking guide recognizes the region as a whole.

Although it is common to think of the Potomac as the dividing line between North and South, the river enabled strong bonds between the Northern Neck and Southern Maryland in the earliest days of the Virginia and Maryland colonies. The river was alive with sails. Family and commercial ties extended across the water. In The Potomac, Frederick Gutheim described what could nearly be called traffic jams of boats and ships and skiffs. Today, one is more likely to encounter tour boats and pleasure craft.

Local citizens and officials are planning a walking route for the PHT up the Northern Neck to Fredericksburg, then north to Prince William County. For now, rather than describing a roadside walking route for the PHT in the region, this guidebook offers up a guide to hiking trails on the Northern Neck and Fredericksburg area. This chapter of *Potomac Heritage Trail, A Hiker's Guide* has a slightly different format than other chapters. Rather than describing a route, it describes parks and natural areas that have hiking trails and walking opportunities. Also, website addresses and phone numbers are included with the information on each hiking area.

Two online resources will be very helpful in planning sojourns to the region. The Virginia Department of Conservation & Recreation has fact sheets on the parks and "natural area preserves" in its system. Each one that appears in this guide can be accessed through www.dcr.state.va.us, then going to the list of parks or natural area preserves. The privately owned and operated natural and heritage areas also have web sites that provide details on park hours and programs. Often they provide stories on how the land was preserved—stories that are themselves part of the Potomac's heritage now.

A second resource is www.northernneck.com, a website focusing on the region. The pages offer a portal to local chambers of commerce, history and travel information.

For those who want to travel this part of the trail corridor under their own power, the best options are by bicycle, using the Tidewater Potomac Heritage Bicycling Route published by Adventure Cycling Association, and by boat using charts and guides that follow the shoreline, part of the evolving Potomac River Water Trail. See the Resources section for contact information.

Several trails in this guide have opened only in the past few years. Other gems, like James Monroe's Birthplace, are awaiting improvements. Still other opportunities lie dormant for lack of energy, funding or will. Such is the case with an abandoned rail line from Dahlgren to Fredericksburg, a beautiful, historic, intact corridor awaiting a critical level of public appreciation.

New segments are being developed in Northern Virginia that will improve the hiking experience. Before embarking on a long-distance hike, contact the local managing agency for maps and updates.

1 Caledon Natural Area

Bald eagles are the big attraction at Caledon, a 2,579-acre park which is designated a National Natural Landmark. Five hiking trails are open year-round, taking hikers through ecologically rich marshlands and woodlands. The 3.5 mile Boyd's Hole Trail leading to the Potomac River is the most popular of the trails. Because human traffic disturbs the park's summer population of roosting and foraging eagles, the Boyd's Hole Trail is open only from October 1 through March 31.

Caledon is a destination hike—worthy of a long drive for a day hike. There are breathtaking views of the Potomac and, for the lucky, many glimpses of bald eagles. The park offers a variety of exceptional interpretive programs and guided hikes, many for children.

TRIP PLANNER

Trailhead: Caledon is 20 miles east of Fredericksburg, Va., on Route 218. From Fredericksburg, take Route 218 east from Route 301, then Route 206 west for four miles to Route 218, then west about one mile.

Restrooms: Available in the visitor center.
Camping: Day use only, but limited camping available for groups with advance registration.
Provisions: Stock up for your picnic en route to the park. Vending machines in visitor center offer snacks.
Website: www.dcr.state.va.us.
Telephone: (540) 663-3861.

2 George Washington's Birthplace

Visitors to Popes Creek Plantation are often struck by its isolation. Tucked into a cove on Popes Creek at the confluence with the Potomac, Washington's birthplace illustrates how far removed the first colonists were from England and Europe. And as a memorial to the first president,

it is the opposite of the more familiar grand and elegant monuments. Through the place it is possible to understand the earliest influences of a person most of us know only through legends.

One fact of early 18th century life we can only imagine now is the role of the Potomac River as a highway. In the early days of Virginia, the Potomac along the Northern Neck was busy with ships and skiffs. Tobacco, wheat and corn were shipped "back home" to Britain, and goods from Britain shipped to the plantations. Local commerce was so plantation-centered that few towns emerged as commercials centers—all eyes and attention were on the waters of the Potomac, the Rappahannock and the many navigable smaller rivers and creeks.

For hikers, the grounds are explored on foot via network of paths. There is also a one-mile nature trail. Popes Creek Plantation offers short walks punctuated with long pauses to watch the water and contemplate the interpretive exhibits about colonial tobacco plantations and how they shaped Virginia and the southern colonies.

TRIP PLANNER

Trailhead: George Washington's Birthplace is 38 miles east of Fredericksburg, Va. Take Route 3 south 35 miles to Route 204; turn left and follow to the park entrance.

Restrooms: Visitor center.

Provisions: None available at the site, but there is a picnic area with a memorable view.

Camping: At nearby Westmoreland State Park.

Website: www.nps.gov/gewa.

Telephone: (804) 224-1732.

3 Stratford Hall Plantation

The birthplace of Robert E. Lee is one of the finer "history hiking" opportunities in the Potomac Heritage Trail corridor. Whether walking in the West Garden, wandering the grounds amid the outbuildings scattered over the acres, or hiking the nature trails through Stratford's woodlands, you get to experience this piece of history on foot and outdoors (as well as all there is to enjoy indoors). Although in history Generals Lee and Washington are from entirely different epochs, their families are both rooted along the Potomac River in the early 18th century and separated by only a few miles of shoreline.

TRIP PLANNER

Trailhead: Stratford Hall Plantation is 45 miles east of Fredericksburg, Va. Take Route 3 south 42 miles to Route 214; turn left and follow to the entrance. Stratford is open daily.

Restrooms: On site.

Provisions: Fried chicken, crab cakes and other Southern fare in the log cabin Plantation Dining room.

Camping: Nearby Westmoreland State Park.

Website: www.stratfordhall.org

Telephone: (804) 493-8038 (weekdays), (804) 493-8371 (weekends, holidays).

4 Westmoreland State Park

There are several miles of hiking trails at Westmoreland. The main attraction for many is the chance to hunt for fossils, whale bones and shark teeth along the Potomac River at the foot of Horsehead Cliffs—remnants of the Miocene Sea. Westmoreland is situated between the birthplaces of George Washington and Robert E. Lee. The cabins and campsites make the park the perfect base from which to explore Lee's Stratford Hall, Washington's Popes Creek Plantation and other area attractions. It's also a fine place to just hang out on the beach, take an afternoon hike and rent a kayak or canoe.

TRIP PLANNER

Trailhead: Westmoreland State Park is 40 miles east of Fredericksburg, Va. Take Route 3 south 40 miles to the entrance. There are picnic tables, boat rentals and a boat launch.

Restrooms: Available at the beach and camping areas.

Provisions: Snack bar.

Camping: Cabins and campsites.

Website: www.dcr.state.va.us

Telephone: (804) 439-8821.

5 Bush Mill Stream Natural Area Preserve

Bush Mill Stream is a brackish tidal creek that serves as a nursery for blue crab, yellow perch and other estuarine species. Within 105 acres, the preserve includes varied habitat, from hillside hardwood/pine forest to swamp to wetland that interact directly with the stream. Leading to the creek are a series of steep ravines, some containing springs that are home to a rare amphipod—a tiny shrimp-like creature that dwells primarily in groundwater. The developed trail system is limited to the half-mile Deep Landing Trail, which in a short distance traverses the complexity of the preserve's topography and habitat, ending at Bush Mill Stream. About midway along the path is the Heron Loop, a quarter-mile stroll to an overlook offering the patient, quiet walker a bird's eye view of this great bird in stillness and action.

TRIP PLANNER

Trailhead: From Kilmarnock, Va., travel north on Route 3 about 7 miles to Lancaster. Turn right (north) on Route 600 and go 1.5 miles to Route 201. Bear right (north) on Route 201 and go about 6.5 miles to Route 642. A brick church is on the right. Turn right (east) on Route 642 and go 0.3 mile to the preserve entrance on the left. The parking area is 0.1 mile down the gravel entrance road.

Restrooms, Camping: None.
Website: www.dcr.state.va.us/dnh/bushmill.htm

6 Hughlett Point Natural Area Preserve

Situated on a peninsula in the Chesapeake Bay, Hughlett Point Natural Area has 204 acres of undeveloped beach, dunes and forest. It is home to river otters, gray foxes and an array of summering and shorebirds and waterfowl, including the American black duck and tundra swan. The forest provides important nesting habitat for songbirds. About

the only things unnatural is the interpretive signage that enriches the experience of the boardwalk and observation platforms. The trail system sidles through upland forest, marshes and the beach. The site may be periodically closed for resource management purposes; updates are posted on the website below.

TRIP PLANNER
Trailhead: From Kilmarnock, Va., by traveling north on Route 200 about 4 miles to Route 606. Turn right (east) onto Route 606 and go about 2 miles to Route 605. Turn right (south) on Route 605 and go about 2 miles to the preserve parking area on the left.
Restrooms, Camping: None.
Website: www.dcr.state.va.us/dnh/hughlett.htm

7 Voorhees Nature Preserve

This preserve along the Rappahannock River is best known as a roosting and nesting site for bald eagles. It also represents an interesting conservation experience. Donated to The Nature Conservancy in 1994 by the Voorhees family, the preserve is adjacent to Westmoreland Berry Farm, which provides passage into the preserve. Visitors park at the farm store, wander the trails and watch for eagles, then return to the farm for a snack and pick-your-own fruits and vegetables. With 729 acres, the preserve offers lots of room to lose yourself in the Rappahannock's scenery and solitude. Westmoreland Berry Farm makes re-entry into civilization gradual and enjoyable. Forget dinner and a movie for that first date—take a hike and pick some berries.

TRIP PLANNER

Trailhead: From Fredericksburg, take Route 3 east into King George County. Watch for the Route 301 intersection. Beyond this intersection, continue for 7 miles on Route 3. Just after Westmoreland County line, look for Westmoreland Berry Farm sign. Turn right onto Route 634, following signs for berry farm. Park in lot at the farm.

Restrooms: Westmoreland Berry Farm.

Provisions: Shop for vegetables and berries at the Westmoreland Berry Farm store. Trail maps are available there, too.

Camping: None.

Website:
www.nature.org/wherewework/northamerica/states/virginia/preserves/

8 Historic Fredericksburg

How's this for hiking? Leave the car behind and take the train to Fredericksburg. Both Amtrak and the Virginia Railway Express stop in downtown Fredericksburg. You can easily spend an entire weekend wandering through the historic district and along the Rappahannock River, where Ferry Farm lies on the opposite shore. There are restaurants and watering holes with outdoor seating. While indoors you will find museums, galleries and other cultural attractions, including George Washington's boyhood home. Stay at a B&B or hotel in town, rent a boat or bicycle; and you'll never miss the car.

TRIP PLANNER

Trailhead: By car, all roads south from greater Washington, D.C., lead to Fredericksburg. For a unique weekend, take the train and go carless for a weekend.

Website: http://www.fredericksburgvirginia.net for lodging and attractions; see Resources below for train information.

9 Belle Isle State Park

Few parks anywhere can boast seven miles of waterfront. Belle Isle State Park has that and 733 acres. It has the Rappahannock River, wild areas, an elegant reproduction colonial mansion available to guests, hiking trails, canoe and bicycle rentals, saltwater fishing, two guest houses, wildlife and dark skies at night. It is an unusual and distinctive park, the first one purchased with funds from a $95 million bond created in 1992. Guided, interpretive canoe trips are available.

TRIP PLANNER

Trailhead: From Kilmarnock, Va., take Route 3 west to Lively, then left on Route 201. Go three miles, then turn right on Route 354. Go three miles, then turn left on Route 683 and proceed to park entrance.

Restrooms: Yes.

Provisions: A snack bar and tackle shop; boat and canoe rentals. No groceries available at the park.

Camping, Lodging: The Bel Air Mansion, the two houses in the Bel Air Overnight Area, and the Bel Air Guest House are available for rent. See the park's website for details.

Website: www.dcr.state.va.us/parks/bellisle.htm

10 Hickory Hollow Natural Area Preserve

Three and a half miles of footpaths wind through 254 acres of forest owned by the Northern Neck Audubon Society. The preserve is home to a variety of breeding bird species and more than 500 plant species. Hickory Hollow contains a number of plants that are rare for lowland forests. There are picnic tables and well-marked trails. Trail maps and interpretive brochures are available at the trailhead kiosk.

TRIP PLANNER

Trailhead: Hickory Hollow is easy to locate, situated behind Lancaster High School on Regina Road, less than a half mile off Route 3 in Kilmarnock.

Restroom, Camping: None.

Website: www.northernneckaudubon.org.

11 Dameron Marsh Natural Area Preserve

The 316-acre Dameron Marsh Natural Area Preserve contains one of the most significant wetlands on the Chesapeake Bay for marsh-bird communities. Its pristine beach habitat is important for the federally threatened northeastern beach tiger beetle. Dameron Marsh supports impressive salt marsh communities, sand beach and upland forest habitats. Virginia Department of Conservation and Recreation is partnering with The Nature Conservancy to develop long-term conservation management plans for the site. The site may be periodically closed for resource management purposes, and access is coordinated by DCR staff. Before visiting, contact Rebecca Wilson, Chesapeake Bay Region Steward, Department of Conservation and Recreation, Division of Natural Heritage, Richmond, VA (804) 445-9117.

TRIP PLANNER
Trailhead: In Northumberland County.
Restrooms, Camping: None.
Website: www.dcr.state.va.us/dnh/dameron.htm

12 Fredericksburg and Spotsylvania National Military Park

The park is a system of sites commemorating four major actions of the U.S. Civil War: the Battle of Fredericksburg, December 11-13, 1862; the Chancellorsville Campaign (encompassing the battles of Chancellorsville, Second Fredericksburg, and Salem Church), April 27-May 6, 1863; the Battle of the Wilderness, May 5-6, 1864; and the Battle of Spotsylvania Court House, May 8-21, 1864. The website describing the battles and linking the sites together does an exceptional job of providing visitor information. Only two of the sites have visitor centers, but each has trails and walking opportunities. You could make a weekend of walking the battlefields.

TRIP PLANNER
Trailhead: The park is in and west (up to 12 miles) of Fredericksburg.
Lodging and Provisions: See Fredericksburg listing.
Website: www.nps.gov/frsp
Telephone: Fredericksburg Battlefield Visitor Center (540) 373-6122;
    Chancellorsville Visitor Center (540) 786-2880.

13 George Washington's Ferry Farm

Across the Rappahannock River from Fredericksburg, Ferry Farm was purchased by Augustine Washington in 1738 and is the place where George Washington spent his formative years. Now it is mostly forested with a mixture of oak, alder, beech, dogwood, gum, buttonbush, locust, maple, tulip poplar, walnut, and ash. They grow thickly on the river slopes, providing cover for a diverse bird population. In spring, the river bottomland is colorful with wildflowers.

TRIP PLANNER
Trailhead: Ferry Farm is directly across the Rappahannock River
    from Fredericksburg on Kings Highway; 268 Kings Highway,
    Fredericksburg, VA 22405.
Restrooms, Water: Available.
Lodging, Provisions: In Fredericksburg, just across the river.
Website: www.kenmore.org
Telephone: (540) 370-0732.

14 Colonial Beach Historic District

Colonial Beach is a small beach town on the shores of the Potomac. In the late nineteenth century, Victorian houses sprang up to serve as vacation homes and several hotels hosted the influx of summer tourists. The town's website boasts Alexander Graham Bell as an early resident. It's a fine little town for taking a stroll, a swim or a siesta. Especially recommended is a hike through the town's historic district.

TRAILHEAD
Trailhead: Colonial Beach is 40 miles southeast of Fredericksburg,
    reach via Route 301, then Route 205.
Lodging, Provisions: See website.
Website: www.colonialbeachva.net
Telephone: (804) 224-0732 for the tourism office.

15 Village of Kinsale

Established in 1706, Kinsale is the oldest port on the Virginia side of the Potomac. A self-guided Kinsale village walking tour begins at the Kinsale Museum. The museum traces the village's history from its beginnings as a colonial port, through the bustling steamboat days to the present. Northern Neck Eco Tours offers kayak tours of the ecosystem of the Chesapeake Bay, Potomac and Rappahannock Rivers, and the numerous tributary creeks in the region. The company offers kayaking trips ranging from a half-day to overnight with lodging at a B&B. Port Kinsale Maritime Museum focuses on the traditions and heritage of the Chesapeake Bay's workboats. Its flagship the skipjack "Virginia W." is one of the oldest remaining Virginia-built skipjacks.

Trailhead: Kinsale is about 65 miles southeast of Fredericksburg. Take Route 3 to Route 203.

Lodging, Provisions: Available in town; see website.

Website: www.westmoreland-county.org

Telephone: (804) 472-3001.

16 Reedville

Reedville is known as a fisherman's town. It is home to a thriving menhaden commercial fishing industry and sport fishing charters. The Reedville Fisherman's Museum is located in the center of the town's historic district. The museum houses a collection of traditional Chesapeake Bay work boats. While at the museum, pick up a copy of the Reedville Walking Tour brochure. The tour describes the turn-of-the-century Victorian homes which line Main Street.

TRIP PLANNER

Trailhead: Reedville is 85 miles southeast of Fredericksburg along Route 360.

Lodging, Provisions: See website.

Website: www.northernneck.org for the Northern Neck Tourism Council.

17 James Monroe's Birthplace

The 75 acre forested area had been largely ignored as a public space for many years. Westmoreland County, which owns the site, commissioned a master plan for creating a modest memorial and public open space for hiking, nature study and education. The plan received an award from the American Society of Landscape Architects. Those plans will unfold over several years, but already the site provides a canoe launch and a quiet, pleasant setting for a hike along an old road to Monroe Creek. A marker identifies the former home site, and there is a modest memorial to the fifth U.S. President.

TRIP PLANNER
Trailhead: James Monroe's Birthplace is in Monroe Hall on Route 205, about 35 miles southeast of Fredericksburg, a few miles from Colonial Beach.
Facilities: There are no facilities at this time.
Website: www.northernneck.org for updates on the plans.

RESOURCES
Amtrak
(800) 872-7245
www.amtrak.com

Fredericksburg Area Tourism
(800) 654-4118

Northern Neck Audubon
www.northernneckaudubon.org

Northern Neck Planning District Commission
www.nnpdc17.org

Northern Neck Tourism Council
www.northernneck.org

Tidewater Potomac Heritage Bicycle Route
Adventure Cycling Association (2004; map with interpretation)
(406) 721-1776
www.adventurecycling.org

Virginia Department of Conservation and Recreation
www.dcr.state.va.us

Virginia Railway Express
(703) 684-0400
www.vre.org

Potomac River Water Trail:
DC to the Chesapeake Bay – 6 Colorful Strip Maps
Virginia Dept. of Conservation and Recreation
(804) 786-5046
www.dcr.state.va.us

TRAIL AND OUTDOOR CONTACTS

I n the Potomac Heritage Trail corridor there are many fine groups dedicated to helping you discover the outdoors. Others are helping to preserve land, create access points to water, and develop new trails. This section puts you in touch with them. It is by no means a comprehensive list. The list does not include specific parks or all the agencies listed in the Resources section of each hike—although a few of the groups below do manage a park or trail. Rather, it is meant to help you find a group you whose activities you can join and whose work you might support.

Accokeek Foundation
3400 Bryan Point Rd.
Accokeek, MD 20607
(301) 283-2113
fax: (301) 283-2049
www.accokeek.org
accofound@accokeek.org

Allegheny Highlands Trail (Md.)
P.O. Box 28
Cumberland, MD 21501
www.ahtmtrail.org

Allegheny Trail Alliance
(888) ATA-BIKE
www.atatrail.org

American Hiking Society
1422 Fenwick Lane
Silver Spring, MD 20910
www.americanhiking.org

Appalachian Trail Conservancy
(304) 535-6331
www.appalachiantrail.org

**Arlington County Department of Parks,
Recreation & Community Resources**
(703) 228-4747
www.co.arlington.va.us/prcr

Blue Ridge Center for Environmental Stewardship
11661 Harpers Ferry Road
Purcellville, VA 20132
(540) 668-7640
www.brces.org

C&O Canal Association
P.O. Box 366
Glen Echo, MD 20812
(301) 983-0825
http://www.candocanal.org

Charles County Division of Park and Recreation
www.charlescounty.org/pf/pg/parks

**Chesapeake Bay Field Office
Trust for Public Land**
666 Pennsylvania Avenue
Washington, DC 20003
www.tpl.org

**Chesapeake Field Office
Trust for Public Land**
666 Penn. Ave. SE
Washington, DC 20003
(202) 543-7552
www.tpl.org

Community Commons
47 South Carroll Street
Frederick, ME 21701
(301) 662-3000

Conservancy for Charles County
1170 Overlook
Accokeek, MD 20607
(301) 283-2410

DC Heritage Tourism Coalition
www.culturaltourismdc.org

East Coast Greenway Alliance, Inc.
135 Main Street
Wakefield, RI 02879
(401) 798-1706
www.greenway.org

Fairfax County Park Authority
(703) 324-8702
http://www.co.fairfax.va.us/parks/

Fairfax Trails and Streams
www.fairfaxtrails.org

Frederick County Tourism Council
www.fredericktourism.org

Great Falls Trail Blazers
660 Mine Ridge
Great Falls, VA 22066

Greater Washington National Parks Fund
c/o National Park Foundation
11 Dupont Circle Suite 600
Washington, DC 20036-1224

Harpers Ferry Conservancy
P.O. Box 1350
Harpers Ferry, WV 25443
(304) 535-9961
www.harpersferry.org

Keystone Trails Association
www.kta-hike.org
Land Trust of the Eastern Panhandle
P.O. Box 1358
Shepherdstown, WV 25443

Loudoun County Convention & Visitors Association
www.visitloudoun.org

Loudoun County Dept. of Parks, Recreation & Community Services
(703) 777-0343
www.loudoun.gov/prcs/home.htm

Maryland Environmental Trust
(410) 514-7900

Mason Neck Citizens Association
P.O. Box 612
Lorton, VA 22199
(703) 541-3123

National Hispanic Environmental Council
5909 N. Coverdale Way, 3rd Floor
Alexandria, VA 22310
(703) 922-3429

National Maritime Heritage Foundation
236 Massachusetts Ave. NE, Suite 410
Washington, DC 20002
(202) 547-1250
www.nmhf.org

National Park Service, National Capital Region
www.nps.gov/ncro

Northern Neck Land Conservancy
(804) 435-2334

Northern Virginia Conservation Trust Packard Center
4022 Hummer Road
Annandale, VA 22003
www.nvct.org

Northern Virginia Regional Commission
(703) 642-0700
www.novaregion.org

Northern Virginia Regional Park Authority
5400 Ox Road
Fairfax Station, VA 22039
(703) 352-5900
www.nvrpa.org

NPS National Capital-Central
(202) 426.6841
www.nps.gov/nacc

NPS National Capital-East
(202) 690-5185
www.nps.gov/nace

Oxon Hill Bicycle and Trail Club
www.ohbike.org

North Country Trail Association, Pennsylvania Chapter
PO Box 2968
Butler, PA 16001
(724) 287-3382
http://www.northcountrytrail.net

Pennsylvania Environmental Council
130 Locust Street, Suite 200
Harrisburg, PA 17101
www.pecpa.org

Potomac Appalachian Trail Club
118 Park Street SE
Vienna, VA 22180
(703) 242-0693
www.patc.net

Potomac Conservancy
8601 Georgia Avenue, Suite 612
Silver Spring, MD 20910
(301) 608-1188
www.potomac.org

Potomac Heritage Partnership, Inc.
1623 28th Street NW
Washington, DC 20007
(202) 333-4478
php1623@aol.com

Potomac Heritage Trail Association
c/o 7017 Hector Road
McLean, VA 2210
(888) 223-4093
info@potomactrail.org

Potomac Water Trail Association, Inc.
P.O. Box 480
Accokeek, MD 20607

Prince Georges County Division of Parks and Recreation
(301) 454-1740
www.mncppc.org

Prince William County Park Authority
(703) 792-7275
www.pwcparks.org/

Seneca Greenway
www.senecatrail.org/

Saint Mary's County Division of Parks and Recreation
www.co.saint-marys.us/recreate

Student Conservation Association
1800 N. Kent Street Suite 102
Arlington, VA 22209
(703) 524-2441

The Wilderness Society
1615 M Street, N.W.
Washington, DC 20036
(202) 833-2300

Tri-County Council for Southern Maryland
P.O. Box 745
Hughesville, MD 20637
(301) 274-1922
www.tccsmd.org

U.S. Fish & Wildlife Service
www.refuges.fws.gov

Virginia Bicycling Federation
P.O. Box 5621
Arlington, VA 22205
www.vabike.org

Virginia Outdoors Foundation
203 Governor Street, Suite 317
Richmond, VA 23219
(804) 225-2147

Washington Area Bicyclists Association, Inc.
1511 K Street N.W., Suite 1015
Washington, DC 20005
(202) 628-2500
waba@waba.org

Washington Parks and People
Josephine Butler Parks Center
2437 15th Street, NW
Washington, DC 20009
(202) GO-2-PARK
washingtonparks@aol.com

BOOKS OF THE PHT CORRIDOR

L ooking for a guide to trails in Western Maryland? How about lodging along the C&O Canal? Or a water trail map. Below is a list of some of the many resources to help you find yourself in the outdoors or on the river. For armchair travel, or for books to take on your travels, the list below includes a number of books that explore the history, nature and culture of the watershed.

BOOKS

184 miles of adventure: Hikers Guide to the C&O Canal
Mason-Dixon Council Boy Scouts of America
Hagerstown, MD

A Guide to Food and Lodging along the C&O Canal
Chesapeake and Ohio Canal Association, Inc. (1999)
Glen Echo, MD

A Hiker's Guide to the Laurel Highlands Trail
Sierra Club, Pennsylvania Chapter (5th ed.,1991)
Pittsburgh, PA
(412) 561-0203

Western Pennsylvania Conservancy
Pittsburgh, PA
(412) 288-2777

**A Passage through Time and the Mountains:
The Story of the Great Allegheny Passage**
Great Allegheny Press/Shaw-Weil Associates (2002)
(888) ATA-BIKE
www.atatrail.org

**Appalachian Trail Guide to Maryland and
Northern Virginia with Side Trails**
Potomac Appalachian Trail Club (1st ed. 2000)
118 Park Street SE
Vienna, VA 22180
(703) 242-0315
www.patc.net

City within a City: Greater U Street Heritage Trail
by Paul K Williams and Kathryn S. Smith
DC Heritage Tourism Coalition, now called Cultural Tourism DC; (2001)
www.culturaltourismdc.org
(202) 828-WALK

Civil War to Civil Rights: Downtown Heritage Trail
by Richard T. Busch
Howell Press (2001)
Charlottesville, VA
www.howellpress.com

Discovering the Tidal Potomac: A Cruising Guide and Boating Reference
Rick Rhodes
Heron Island Press (2003)

Commoners, Tribute, and Chiefs:
The Development of Algonquian Culture in the Potomac Valley
Stephen R. Potter
University of Virginia Press (1993)

Great Little Walks: A guide to walks on the Great Allegheny Passage
& connecting trails in the Pittsburgh Area
Yvonne Merrill, AE Richardson & Mary Shaw
Great Allegheny Press (2nd Edition 2005))
Shaw-Weil Associates
(888) ATA-BIKE

Hikes in Western Maryland
Potomac Appalachian Trail Club (1st ed. 1997)
118 Park Street SE
Vienna, VA 22180
(703) 242-0315

Images of America: Along the Potomac
Philip Woodworth Ogilvie and the Potomac Water Trail Association
Arcadia Publishing (1999; second printing 2003)
Charleston, SC
www.arcadiapublishing.com

Leaning Sycamores: Natural Worlds of the Upper Potomac
Jack Wennerstrom, Sandy Glover
Johns Hopkins University Press (1996)
Baltimore, MD

Life on the Potomac River
Edwin W. Beitzell
Heritage Books (2003)

Linking Up: Planning Your Traffic-Free Bike Trip between Pittsburgh PA and Washington DC
Mary Shaw and Roy Weil, with mapping by Bill Metzger
Shaw-Weil Associates
414 S. Craig St. PMB 307
Pittsburgh, PA 15213
www.atatrail.org or (888) ATA-BIKE

The C&O Canal Companion
Mike High
The Johns Hopkins University Press (2000)
Baltimore, MD

The Grand Idea: George Washington's Potomac and the Race to the West
Joel Achenbach
Simon & Shuster (2004)
New York

The Great Allegheny Passage Companion: Guide to History and Heritage along the Trail
by William Metzger
The Local History Company (2003)
112 North Woodland Road
Pittsburgh, PA 15232
www.thelocalhistorycompany.com

The Potomac
Frederick Gutheim
John Hopkins University Press
Baltimore, MD

Towpath Guide to the Chesapeake and Ohio Canal: Georgetown Tidelock to Cumberland
Thomas F. Swiftwater Hahn
Harpers Ferry Historical Association
Harpers Ferry, WV

Walk and Bike the Alexandria Heritage Trail: A Guide to Exploring a Virginia Town's Hidden Past
by Pamela J. Cressey, Ph.D., RPA for the Friends of Alexandria Archeology
Capital Books, Inc. (2002)
22841 Quicksilver Drive
Sterling, VA 20166
(703) 661-1531

MAPS OF THE PHT CORRIDOR

Tidewater Potomac Heritage Bicycle Route
Adventure Cycling Association (2004; map with interpretation)
Missoula, MT 59807
(406) 721-1776
www.adventurecycling.org

Guide to Recreation Trails in Northern Virginia
Northern Virginia Regional Commission
(703) 642-0700
www.novaregion.org

**Potomac River Water Trail and the C&O Canal:
Shepherdstown, W. Va. to Potomac Park, Md.**
Jointly by Maryland Dept. of Natural Resources, C & O Canal National
Historical Park, Interstate Commission on the Potomac River Basin,
and West Virginia Department of Natural Resources (2002)
Maryland Dept. of Natural Resources
(410) 260-8778
www.dnr.state.md.us/greenways, and

Interstate Commission on the Potomac River Basin
(301) 984-1908
www.potomacriver.org

**Potomac River and C&O Canal:
Five Colorful Strip Maps Georgetown to Opequon Creek**
Interstate Commission on the Potomac River Basin
(301) 984-1908
www.potomacriver.org

**Potomac River Water Trail:
DC to the Chesapeake Bay – 6 Colorful Strip Maps**
Maryland Dept. of Natural Resources
(410) 260-8778
www.dnr.state.md.us/greenways, and

Virginia Dept. of Conservation and Recreation
(804) 786-5046
www.dcr.state.va.us

Map D: Trails in the Potomac Gorge Area Maryland and Northern Virginia and Cabin John Trail Maryland
Potomac Appalachian Trail Club (2001)
118 Park Street SE
Vienna, VA 22180
(703) 242-0315
www.patc.net